Marcus Garvey

BLACK NATIONALIST LEADER

Black Americans of Achievement

LEGACY EDITION

Marcus Garvey

BLACK NATIONALIST LEADER

Mary Lawler

With additional text written by
John Davenport

Consulting Editor, Revised Edition
Heather Lehr Wagner

Senior Consulting Editor, First Edition
Nathan Irvin Huggins
Director, W.E.B. Du Bois Institute
for Afro-American Research
Harvard University

CHELSEA HOUSE
PUBLISHERS
A Haights Cross Communications Company
Philadelphia

COVER: UNIA leader Marcus Garvey riding in a parade at the First Convention of the Negro Peoples of the World in 1920.

CHELSEA HOUSE PUBLISHERS

VP, NEW PRODUCT DEVELOPMENT Sally Cheney
DIRECTOR OF PRODUCTION Kim Shinners
CREATIVE MANAGER Takeshi Takahashi
MANUFACTURING MANAGER Diann Grasse

Staff for MARCUS GARVEY

EXECUTIVE EDITOR Lee Marcott
ASSISTANT EDITOR Alexis Browsh
PRODUCTION EDITOR Noelle Nardone
PHOTO EDITOR Sarah Bloom
SERIES AND COVER DESIGNER Keith Trego
LAYOUT 21st Century Publishing and Communications, Inc.

A Haights Cross Communications ✦ Company

www.chelseahouse.com

First Printing

9 8 7 6 5 4 3 2 1

Library of Congress Cataloging-in-Publication Data

Lawler, Mary.
   Marcus Garvey: Black nationalist leader/Mary Lawler; with additional text by John Davenport.
      p. cm.—(Black Americans of achievement)
Includes bibliographical references and index.
   ISBN 0-7910-8159-1 — ISBN 0-7910-8333-0 (pbk.)
   1. Garvey, Marcus, 1887–1940—Juvenile literature. 2. African Americans—Biography—
Juvenile literature. 3. Intellectuals—United States—Biography—Juvenile literature.
4. Universal Negro Improvement Association—Juvenile literature. I. Davenport, John, 1960–
II. Title. III. Series.
E185.97.G3L395 2004
973'.0496073'0092—dc22

                                                                        2004012658

Contents

Introduction

Nearly 20 years ago Chelsea House Publishers began to publish the first volumes in the series called BLACK AMERICANS OF ACHIEVEMENT. This series eventually numbered over a hundred books and profiled outstanding African Americans from many walks of life. Today, if you ask school teachers and school librarians what comes to mind when you mention Chelsea House, many will say—"Black Americans of Achievement."

The mix of individuals whose lives we covered was eclectic, to say the least. Some were well known—Muhammad Ali and Dr. Martin Luther King, Jr, for example. But others, such as Harriet Tubman and Sojourner Truth, were lesser-known figures who were introduced to modern readers through these books. The individuals profiled were chosen for their actions, their deeds, and ultimately their influence on the lives of others and their impact on our nation as a whole. By sharing these stories of unique Americans, we hoped to illustrate how ordinary individuals can be transformed by extraordinary circumstances to become people of greatness. We also hoped that these special stories would encourage young-adult readers to make their own contribution to a better world. Judging from the many wonderful letters we have received about the BLACK AMERICANS OF ACHIEVEMENT biographies over the years from students, librarians, and teachers, they have certainly fulfilled the goal of inspiring others!

Now, some 20 years later, we are publishing 18 volumes of the original BLACK AMERICANS OF ACHIEVEMENT series in revised editions to bring the books into the twenty-first century and make them available to a new generation of young-adult readers. The selection was based on the importance of these figures to American life and the popularity of the original books with our readers. These revised editions have a new full-color design and, wherever possible, we have added color photographs. The books have new features, including quotes from the writings and speeches of leaders and interesting and unusual facts about their lives. The concluding section of each book gives new emphasis to the legacy of these men and women for the current generation of readers.

The lives of these African-American leaders are unique and remarkable. By transcending the barriers that racism placed in their paths, they are examples of the power and resiliency of the human spirit and are an inspiration to readers.

We present these wonderful books to our audience for their reading pleasure.

Lee M. Marcott
Chelsea House Publishers
August 2004

Homecoming

The steamship *Santa Marta* was not scheduled to arrive in Kingston, Jamaica, until the afternoon, but early that Saturday morning crowds had already begun to gather near the pier. Black men and women, young and old, had started to line the streets that led to the capital city's port, eagerly awaiting the return of Marcus Garvey, their beloved leader and countryman. On that day, December 10, 1927, he was still one of the most famous black men in the world.

Twelve years before, at the age of 28, Garvey had left his native island of Jamaica for the United States. Settling in New York, he quickly rose to become a leader of blacks in America and all over the world. He also made some powerful enemies, but none of them seemed to be among the crowds waiting for him to arrive in Kingston.

As the day wore on, the crowd's excitement mounted, until—three hours later than expected—the *Santa Marta* steamed up the channel and into the harbor.

"He's coming! He's coming!" the happy onlookers cried.

On the second deck of the ship stood a 40-year-old man, short and pudgy, with very dark skin and a mustache. He looked dignified even in the cheap, ill-fitting suit that had been issued to him upon his release from a U.S. prison a few weeks earlier.

Once the crowd noticed Garvey on the deck, a deafening cheer went up. The excitement swelled as he made his way down the gangplank and stepped ashore, where he was greeted by officials of the Universal Negro Improvement Association (UNIA), the international black organization that he had founded 13 years earlier. The organization's message of racial pride and unity had spread so quickly and so far that UNIA branches could be found almost everywhere that blacks lived, from Colombia to Canada, from Africa to Australia.

Garvey entered an awaiting car and was driven slowly past the crowds of well wishers, preceded by a small procession of UNIA members and bands marching in colorful costumes. The car traveled slowly through streets thronged with people determined to catch a glimpse of Garvey, who waved and stretched out both arms to shake hands with those who pressed toward him.

"No denser crowd has ever been witnessed in Kingston," reported the *Daily Gleaner*, a local newspaper. At times the crowd was so thick that Garvey's car could barely move. His enthusiastic followers came close to carrying him for the rest of his journey on their shoulders but were stopped by uniformed policemen who lined the route to Liberty Hall, the meeting place of the local UNIA chapter. Garvey had planned on giving a speech in the auditorium of Liberty Hall, but when he reached the building, he saw that thousands of people were jammed inside it and thousands more were crowding the adjacent streets. Determined to have as many people as possible hear his words, he stood on the running board of his car and made a brief speech. He thanked his countrymen for their kind welcome and promised them that "as long as I live, I shall do everything for your advancement, well knowing that the

Marcus Garvey was born in Jamaica and returned to its capital, Kingston, seen here, in 1927. Garvey left Jamaica for New York to form the Universal Negro Improvement Association, an organization that promoted black pride and unity and made Garvey one of the most famous black men of the early twentieth century.

organization which has been established for your uplift will always receive your fullest support."

Then, excited yet exhausted from his travels and his homecoming, Garvey retired to a friend's house to rest and to make plans for the future. He did not suspect that his greatest moment had just passed, that he would never regain the fame and power that had become his only a few years before, when the UNIA had formed the basis of the biggest mass movement in black history. Even so, his dreams of leading his race back to the African continent would live on. In the years to come, many of his goals would be realized, giving future generations cause to remember Marcus Garvey.

2

A Place in the World

Marcus Mosiah Garvey was born on August 17, 1887, in St. Ann's Bay, a picturesque little village on Jamaica's northern coast. The eleventh child of Sarah and Marcus Garvey, he and his older sister Indiana were the only children in the family to reach adulthood; all of the others died during their childhood.

Christened Marcus after his father, Garvey was given the middle name of Mosiah as the result of a compromise. His mother wanted to call him Moses, for she had a hunch that her son would someday lead his people, just as the biblical Moses had led the Jews. His father, not a particularly religious man, favored a less pretentious name. They settled on Mosiah, although most people just called the youngster Mose or, less kindly, Ugly Mug.

Marcus's mother was a gentle, slim, and beautiful woman who was known for being kind and helpful to her neighbors and for working hard to bring up her family. Because her husband found employment only sporadically, the task of supporting and educating the children often fell to her. The daughter of a farming family, she shared a plot of land with her brother, and the proceeds from the crops grown there, along with the cakes and pastries she baked and sold, often supplied the family with its only income.

Marcus's father was different: hard, stern, and stubborn. A skilled stonemason, he cut and shaped white rock for the walls of nearby plantation houses belonging to the island's wealthy estate owners. He worked only when he felt like it. He preferred to spend long hours locked in his private study, reading from his collection of books and magazines. This constant reading kept Marcus's father well informed, and he became known in St. Ann's Bay as the village lawyer—a man whom the other townspeople often went to for advice. He was so respected in the town that everybody—even his wife—called him Mr. Garvey. "My father," Marcus wrote later, "was a man of brilliant intellect and dashing courage. He was unafraid of consequences. . . . He was severe, firm, determined, bold, and strong, refusing to yield even to superior forces if he believed he was right." Yet these qualities eventually caused the downfall of Marcus's father.

The elder Garvey received a newspaper every week for 20 years. Assuming it was a gift from the publisher, he never paid anything for it. When the publisher died, the executors of the estate sent Garvey a bill, which Marcus's father stubbornly ignored. The executors took the matter to court, and Garvey was ordered to pay. He still refused, so the judge sold one of the Garvey family's properties to cover the debt, which had increased because of the court costs. Quarrels with neighbors over boundaries and property rights resulted in other court actions and led to the loss of more Garvey property. Finally, the family was left with only the plot of land on which their home stood.

Stubbornness and pride were character traits that Marcus's father may have gotten from his ancestors. He was a descendant of the Maroons, escaped Jamaican slaves who banded together during the seventeenth and eighttenth centuries to fight the island's British colonial rulers. Located in the Caribbean Sea, part of the group of islands known as the West Indies, Jamaica had been ruled by foreigners for centuries. In 1494, conquistadors arrived from Spain and virtually destroyed the native Arawak Indian population of Jamaica, making the island into a Spanish colony. Spaniards ruled Jamaica until 1655, when it was taken over by the British and briefly became a haven for pirates preying on Spanish shipping. By the late seventeenth century, the West Indies was the center of the lucrative sugar trade, and Britain, France, and the Netherlands constantly warred with each other for control of the islands. As the British began to cover Jamaica with sugar plantations, they were soon faced with the need for a source of cheap labor. Their solution was to import black slaves from Africa for the grueling work of harvesting the sugar cane.

European traders had been kidnapping the people of Africa and selling them into slavery since the 1470s. The traders had originally traveled to Africa in search of gold and treasures, but they soon began buying people instead, dealing with both small coastal tribes and powerful West African nations that sold slaves in return for guns, rum, cloth, and other European goods. During the centuries that the slave trade continued, an estimated 60 to 100 million blacks were taken from Africa and sold into slavery in the New World.

Slave uprisings in the European colonies occurred every now and then over the years, but the fierce Jamaican Maroons preserved their freedom more successfully than did most ex-slave groups. Banding together in the island's inaccessible central highlands, the Maroons developed their own distinct culture. During the 1730s, after 10 years of warfare, the British authorities gave in. They awarded the Maroons tax-free land of their own and gave them the right to govern themselves. Most of the blacks in Jamaica remained slaves, however. In 1833, slavery was finally abolished throughout the British Empire.

The Maroons were escaped British slaves who settled in the Caribbean and fought British colonial rule in the late seventeenth and early eighteenth century. The former slaves, like the man seen here, lived and developed a culture in Jamaica's highlands and eventually were awarded the right to govern themselves and own tax-free land by the British.

The blacks of Jamaica became free, but most did not own land and were poor. By the time of Garvey's birth, they were starting to agitate for better conditions.

Jamaica then had a population of about 600,000. Approximately 80 percent of the island's inhabitants were black. Yet this large segment of the population was primarily a poor laboring class. The whites, who formed only about two percent of the total population, were members of the upper class. The remaining 18 percent of the Jamaicans were mainly "coloreds," people of mixed race who formed the middle class.

GARVEY'S JAMAICA

As the relatively privileged son of a tradesman and landowner, Marcus Garvey knew little of these class boundaries or of racial prejudice. His father's property adjoined that of two white families, and Marcus played with neighborhood children without being concerned about their color. "To me, at home in my early days, there was no difference between white and black," Garvey recalled. "We romped and were happy children playmates together."

Garvey's first lesson in prejudice came when he was a teenager. He recalled later:

> The little white girl who I liked most knew no better than I did myself. We were two innocent fools who never dreamed of a race feeling and problem. . . . At fourteen my little white playmate and I parted. Her parents thought the time had come to separate us and draw the color line. They sent her and another sister to Edinburgh, Scotland, and told her that she was never to try to write or get in touch with me, for I was a "nigger."
>
> It was then that I found for the first time that there was some difference in humanity, and that there were different races, each having its own separate and distinct social life. I did not care about the separation after I was told about it, because I never thought all during my childhood that the girl and the rest of the

children of her race were better than I was; in fact, they used to look up to me. So I simply had no regrets.

Garvey's friendship with white males lasted a little longer but eventually came to a similar end.

At maturity, the black and white boys took different courses in life. I grew up then to see the difference between the races more and more. My schoolmates as young men did not know or remember me any more. Then I realized that I had to make a fight for a place in the world, that it was not so easy to pass on to office and position.

Garvey's fight was helped by his desire to learn. Educated in public grammar schools and by private tutors, he read on his own from the volumes in his father's library. When Garvey was 15, he left school to work full-time as a printer's apprentice in his godfather's shop. This did not mean the end of his education. His godfather was an educated man, and Garvey continued his schooling in the back room of the printing shop, which was filled with old magazines, books, and newspapers.

Always adventurous, Garvey used to sit by the St. Ann's Bay wharf and watch the sailors and dockhands at work, loading ships bound for Germany with pimentos and log wood and for America with citrus, sugar, and rum. Sometimes he would talk with the seamen, whose exciting descriptions of the ports and towns they visited gave him a keen desire to see the world.

At 18, Garvey moved to Kingston, Jamaica's capital, and went to work in his uncle's print shop. Within two years he was a master printer and foreman at one of the island's largest firms. This experience in the printing business proved to be invaluable later in his life, when he started the series of newspapers and journals that became such an important part of the organizations he founded. Garvey's time in Kingston was even more important for the exposure it gave him to the political ideas of the day. When he first arrived in Kingston, he was immediately attracted by the noisy street debates— an informal method of discussing current issues and events. Having no experience in such discussions, his first attempts at adding his own opinions met with a curt "Country boy, shut your mouth!"

Garvey became determined to learn the art of public speaking. He spent his Sundays visiting various churches, listening to the oratorical techniques of Kingston's most popular preachers. Garvey then practiced these skills by reading aloud passages from a schoolbook while experimenting with gestures in front of a mirror. He also carried a pocket dictionary with him and studied it to expand his vocabulary. Caught up in his own studies, he still found time to teach debating techniques to young people. As a friend recalled, "He was always busy, planning and doing something for the underprivileged youth. Uplift work we called it."

During his years in Kingston, Garvey became fully aware of the unfairness of the racial divisions in Jamaican society. "I started to take an interest in the politics of my country," Garvey said, "and then I saw the injustice done to my race because it was black, and I became dissatisfied on that account." He understood that blacks had little chance of overcoming the poverty that was so common among them.

One incident in particular triggered his awareness. On the afternoon of January 14, 1907, an earthquake and fire destroyed much of Kingston. The disaster caused a scarcity of food and goods that, in turn, drove up prices. The city's ill-paid laborers soon had barely enough money to feed themselves. The workers of the printing company where Garvey was employed protested this situation by striking for higher wages. As a foreman, Garvey was in a management position and was not obligated to go out on strike with his men, but he believed the workers' cause was just and joined the strike, even though his employers offered him a salary increase if he would stay on the job.

The strike eventually failed, however. The printing companies brought in new employees content to work for low wages, while the treasurer of the workers' organization ran off with their union money. Workers' organizations, Garvey discovered, were often an ineffective tool for improving the conditions under which blacks lived and worked. Maintaining unity among workers was difficult on an overcrowded island, where huge numbers of desperate, unemployed men competed for meager, low-paying jobs.

Garvey lost his job after the strike was over and went to work at the government printing office. By this time he had already begun to realize that his printing work in Kingston was not really his main interest. In 1909, when he was 22, Garvey became active in Kingston's intellectual circles as a member of the National Club. Organized by a local lawyer to fight the problems caused by Britain's rule of Jamaica, the National Club campaigned for political candidates and put out a publication called *Our Own*. Working on the publication provided Garvey with his first experience in newspaper publishing and prompted him to put out his own periodical at this time. *Garvey's Watchman* soon failed.

By his early 20s, Garvey had become deeply immersed in political activities and efforts to improve the status of Jamaican blacks. He needed more money to support his interest in organizational work—more than he could hope to raise in Jamaica. Many West Indians were going to Central and South America to look for work, and Garvey decided he might find a better-paying job abroad. Thus, in 1910, at the age of 23, he set out for Costa Rica.

3

Doomed to Lead

When Garvey sailed from Kingston in 1910, he intended to work for a short time, save some money, and then go back to Jamaica to continue the struggle for black political rights. He knew that his people would need strong leadership if they were to break their shackles of inequality and poverty. His plans for a quick return to Jamaica changed, however, when he discovered the conditions that blacks labored under in Latin American countries. What he saw there shocked him.

In Costa Rica, Garvey took a job on a banana plantation owned by the United Fruit Company. This giant U.S. firm controlled much of the fruit production in Latin America and was rapidly clearing land for new plantations. As a timekeeper, Garvey kept track of the hours worked by company employees, many of them black West Indians like himself. The workers battled daily to drain swamps while contending with snakes and other wild animals. They worked long hours for low wages, and their money often disappeared into the pockets of petty thieves or dishonest bankers.

Distressed by the plantation workers' suffering, Garvey began a crusade to improve their working conditions. Many of the West Indians were citizens of islands controlled by Britain and were entitled to British protection. The British had close ties with the nations of Central America, and their consulates had a strong amount of influence with the local governments. Garvey therefore decided to bring the workers' plight to the attention of the British consulate in the nearby city of Puerto Limón. To Garvey's dismay the consul showed no interest in the matter and said the British government could do nothing to help the men. It was clear to Garvey that white officials like the consul did not value the lives of black people.

Garvey remained in Puerto Limón, working on the docks with other poorly paid black laborers. Again, he tried to organize the workers. He started a newspaper called *La Nacionale* (*The National*), which agitated for workers' rights and encouraged blacks to demand fairer treatment. He received little support. The mainly illiterate laborers were unable to read his articles in *La Nacionale.* Most were too busy trying to feed themselves to get involved in a political movement. After a short while in Puerto Limón, Garvey decided to see what he could accomplish elsewhere.

Leaving Costa Rica, Garvey traveled to Nicaragua, Colombia, Venezuela, and other Latin American nations. He found West Indian migrant workers in all of these countries, men who had fled the poverty of their own islands only to find nothing but backbreaking work abroad.

In Panama, thousands of blacks were helping to build the nearly completed canal that the U.S. Army Corps of Engineers was constructing to link the Atlantic and Pacific oceans. Many workers caught malaria and other deadly tropical diseases in the steaming Panamanian jungles. Black workers did much of the heavy excavating labor on the 50-mile length of the canal,

Garvey moved to Costa Rica in 1910 to quickly raise some money by working on a banana plantation, like the one shown here, owned by the United Fruit Company. He discovered that working conditions in Costa Rica were even worse than those in Jamaica, and he began a campaign to organize black workers and improve their working conditions.

but they were poorly paid. Their white co-workers lived in separate camps and were treated much better.

In the tobacco fields and copper mines of Ecuador, Garvey discovered more West Indian migrants working in wretched conditions. Again and again, he met with the islanders, heard their complaints, and tried to organize the men into workers' associations. None of the British consulates in the countries he visited would listen to his appeals for help. They always insisted that they could not risk upsetting their friendly relations with the local governments.

After campaigning unsuccessfully for two years to improve the lot of the West Indian workers, Garvey grew discouraged. Wherever he went, he was harassed by government authorities, who viewed him as a dangerous subversive. Finally, in 1912, worn out from a bout with malaria, he returned to Jamaica.

Back home again, his health restored, Garvey renewed his efforts to help his scattered countrymen. In Kingston he found many other people who were concerned about the welfare of relatives working overseas. Garvey organized a delegation to bring the migrant workers' problems to the attention of the governor of Jamaica, the head of the island's colonial administration. Again, Garvey received a cold welcome. The governor told the delegation that if conditions were so bad abroad, then the workers should return to Jamaica. "Return to do what?" Garvey asked, for the reason the men had left Jamaica was that they could not find work at home. The governor made no reply.

Garvey was not defeated. Jamaica, he knew, was only a small part of the British Empire, whose sprawling domain included the modern-day countries Ireland, India, Pakistan, Kenya, Uganda, Barbados, and many other parts of Europe, Asia, Africa, and the West Indies. He believed that in London, where British colonial policy was decided, he might find people who could help the West Indians. Garvey did not have the money for a ticket to England, but his sister, who was working as a nanny in London, sent him the fare. In 1912, at the age of 23, Garvey sailed for England.

LEARNING AND LIVING IN BRITAIN

During his stay in London, Garvey learned much about the conditions experienced by blacks around the world. On the

London docks, where he worked to support himself, Garvey spoke with black seamen from the West Indies, Africa, and the United States. Hearing the sailors describe the indignities blacks endured in other countries, Garvey concluded that no matter where they lived, the people of his race shared a common bond of suffering. Whether they were a minority class or the major racial group in their country made no difference; blacks everywhere had to obey discriminatory laws and accept unfair working conditions.

Although Garvey put in long days on the docks, he still found time to attend classes in law and philosophy at Birkbeck College, a school for working-class people in London. Here he studied the ideas of important thinkers, from the ancient Greek philosophers Socrates and Plato to black scholars of his own time.

Garvey also spent many hours in London's public libraries poring through books on the history and culture of his African ancestors. He read with pride about the Ghana, Mali, and Songhai kingdoms, which centuries earlier had ruled large parts of central and western Africa. Having been taught that Africa's inhabitants had always been poor, primitive tribal folk, Garvey was delighted to learn that advanced civilizations had flourished on the continent long before the Europeans arrived in the fifteenth century. The Africans' magnificent art and music and highly developed political institutions and religious traditions had been virtually ignored by white society.

The heyday of the great African kingdoms had long since passed, however. In Garvey's time, Africa was dominated by European nations. During the nineteenth century, Great Britain, France, Germany, Belgium, Portugal, and Italy had competed against each other to slice up the continent into colonies. Representatives of the European powers met at the Berlin Conference of 1884–85 to establish the boundaries of their colonial states. The only countries that remained in black control were Liberia, a West African nation founded by black immigrants from the

United States, and the ancient east African kingdom of Ethiopia. The European nations justified their occupation of Africa by claiming that they were bringing civilization and Christianity to godless and backward people, the "heathen savages" of the "dark continent." (For additional information about the European occupation of Africa, enter "colonialism in Africa" in any search engine and browse the sites listed.)

The foreign powers' domination of Africa angered Garvey. In London he met many other blacks who shared his views. The large metropolitan city attracted students and intellectuals from around the British Empire who, like Garvey, wanted to be near the center of political activity. London also hosted many international conventions. One of them, held 12 years earlier, brought together delegates representing black communities in England, the West Indies, and the United States to discuss how to promote pan-Africanism.

Formed in the late 1800s, the pan-African movement held as its ideal the belief that blacks throughout the world were one people and that Africa was their common homeland. The members of the movement were devoted to establishing African nations that would be governed by blacks. The leading writers of the pan-African movement—Henry McNeal Turner, Edward Wilmot Blyden, and J.E. Casely Hayford—had a strong influence on Garvey. More and more he came to believe that blacks throughout the world must unite and wrest Africa from its colonial occupiers.

In 1913, Garvey met Duse Mohammed Ali, the half-Egyptian, half-black publisher of the *African Times and Orient Review*, a journal committed to fighting for the rights of the native peoples in African and Asian colonies. Ali took a liking to the much-traveled Jamaican dockworker and hired him as a messenger. Working for the journal allowed Garvey to continue his political education and to become familiar with the leading spokesmen of the international black community, many of whom wrote for the paper. Garvey himself had one piece published in the journal. In the article, Garvey voiced a demand for greater black participation in the Jamaican government, and he predicted that the West Indians would one day help to unite the race into a mighty empire.

Taking a break from his work, writing, and studies, Garvey traveled around Europe, visiting many of those countries whose colonial administrations were supposedly bringing enlightenment to the African people. At the time of Garvey's visit, the political climate in Europe was tense. The major powers had divided into hostile camps and were spending heavily to build up their military forces. Within a year, Great Britain, France, Italy, and Russia would be fighting a horrifyingly destructive war with Germany, Austria-Hungary, and Turkey. This conflict, which began in August 1914, would be known as the Great War, or World War I.

After his tour of Europe, Garvey returned to England, probably in late 1913. He may have visited more English cities, finding work where he could. His wanderings soon came to an end, for he found a book that stopped him in his tracks and burned its way into his soul. The book was *Up from Slavery*, and the author was Booker T. Washington, the most influential black leader in the United States. Born a slave in Virginia in 1856, Washington had gained his freedom during the Civil War. Afterward he worked his way through school and became a respected educator. He was especially famous as the founder of the Tuskegee Institute, an all-black school of higher learning in Alabama. In 1901 he published his autobiography, *Up from Slavery*. In the book, Washington urged the members of his race to work hard, save money, and improve themselves through education. Once educated, Washington envisioned blacks thriving in agriculture, first as farm managers but later as farmers in their own right. He opposed public protests against racial intolerance because he believed they would increase hostilities between blacks and whites. Instead, what Washington advocated was a form of race relations known as accommodation:

After reading Booker T. Washington's book *Up From Slavery*, Garvey was inspired to become a leader of his race and formed the Universal Negro Improvement Association. The most influential black leader of the late nineteenth and early twentieth century, Washington, seen here (seated) in 1902, with his secretary Emmet J. Scott, advocated the improvement of the black race through hard work and education.

blacks should, at least for the time being, accommodate white interests and prejudice. This would avoid conflict long enough to give blacks a chance to advance. Eventually, Washington believed, blacks would be fully accepted by whites and would share equally in the benefits of American society.

Washington's ideas had a profound effect on Garvey's thinking. After reading *Up from Slavery*, he realized he had found his

Booker T. Washington

Marcus Garvey's insistence on self-reliance as the key to black advancement was patterned in large part on the socioeconomic model developed by Booker T. Washington. Both men believed sincerely in the uplifting power of black investment in industry and agriculture and the resulting financial benefits. The two leaders also agreed on the central role played by education in creating an entrepreneurial spirit among black Americans. Garvey corresponded regularly with Washington and admired him greatly; he even went so far as to advocate the creation of a Jamaican version of Washington's Tuskegee Institute. This man, who Garvey strove to emulate, knew the potential for liberation that came with economic self-sufficiency.

Born in 1856 into a world of slavery as the property of a Virginia planter, Washington accepted agriculture as the black man's lot and came to see it as the best hope for true racial uplift. He became convinced that the road to genuine, lasting freedom began in the fields and workshops rather than in the halls of government. Consequently, Washington encouraged black Americans to educate themselves in the agricultural and industrial arts. He envisioned the knowledge gained in such pursuit being applied in an effort to carve out a niche for blacks in the larger national economy and eventually in society in general.

After struggling to get an education at Hampton Institute, Washington took the bold step of designing his own agricultural school—the Tuskegee Institute —in Alabama in 1881. He planned to train a generation of independent black workers and owners. Washington urged blacks to accommodate rather than challenge white interests and to work for black advancement within the white power structure while remaining separate from it. He advocated this form of "separate but equal" socioeconomic arrangement until his death in 1915. This worldview cost Washington dearly in terms of standing among mainstream black leaders at the time, but it won him the unwavering respect of Marcus Garvey, so much so that Garvey's widow once remarked, "Booker T. Washington was the idol of Marcus Garvey."

purpose in life. "My doom—if I may so call it—of being a race leader dawned on me," he recalled later. The book prompted him to ask many disturbing questions: "Where is the black man's Government? Where is his President, his country, and his ambassador, his army, his navy, his men of big affairs?" He promised himself that he would win these things for his people.

UNIA

Filled with great dreams, Garvey made a resolution: "I was determined that the black man would not continue to be kicked about by all the other races and nations of the world. I could not remain in London anymore. My brain was afire." He packed his bags and took passage on a ship bound for Jamaica. Garvey arrived home on July 15, 1914, and immediately began to contact people whom he had worked with in the past. Seventeen days later he formed the Universal Negro Improvement and Conservation Association and African Communities League. The association's title was soon shortened, and it became known as the UNIA. Garvey was appointed president and traveling commissioner (chief recruiter) of the Kingston-based organization. Among the UNIA's officers was Amy Ashwood, a young woman who would serve for many years as Garvey's secretary.

The UNIA's purpose was to unite Jamaica's black population behind a spirit of racial pride and a program of educational and economic opportunity. Furthermore, the UNIA vowed to work for the establishment of independent black-ruled nations in Africa. This great dream could only be achieved, Garvey said, when blacks from around the world joined together and demanded that Africa be freed from colonial rule. Garvey intended the UNIA to be the standard-bearer of international black protest; his organization would force the world's governments to take notice of black unrest.

These great plans would all take time. From the start the UNIA had high ideals but limited funds. Membership dues raised only a small amount of money, and the organization depended on volunteer work. Garvey realized he had to address the immediate needs of Jamaica's poor to gain their support. The UNIA tried to attract recruits by offering a limited form of health insurance. The main thrust of Garvey's program was to promote learning among the ill-educated peasants and workers. Most of these people saw little need for education, knowing they were destined to spend their lives laboring in the fields or on the docks. The UNIA planned to change this outlook.

As his organization's traveling commissioner, Garvey visited many towns and villages in Jamaica in search of new members. Though many people listened to him, few were ready to join the UNIA, and fewer still had any organizational talents. Garvey had no qualms about pointing out his people's shortcomings, admitting that most of them were "unfit for good society." Like Booker T. Washington, he believed that until the black workers became committed to self-improvement, they would be looked down upon by whites. He often used his own struggle to educate himself as an example for others. He told one audience: "I came from surroundings not better than many of you, but my mind lifted me out of my surroundings." In the books of his father and godfather he had found the inspiration to become more than a common dockworker, and he had set his sights on becoming a leader of poor and oppressed people. "Nobody helped me toward that objective," he asserted, "except my own mind and God's good will."

To help his people follow in his footsteps, Garvey organized lectures, debates, speaking contests, adult-education classes, entertainments, and religious meetings. He also called for the establishment of colleges and vocational schools to allow all qualified students to attain higher education. The one special project that consumed Garvey was his idea for a school modeled on the Tuskegee Institute in Alabama. Booker

T. Washington's all-black school was known as an industrial college because it taught students the advanced skills they needed to pursue careers in a trade or business. Among the professors at Tuskegee was George Washington Carver, the agricultural scientist who had helped restore the economy of the American South after the Civil War. Carver had discovered many new uses for peanuts, soybeans, sweet potatoes, cotton, and other crops grown in the region. Garvey dreamed of building a school based on Tuskegee, one that would attract men like Carver and gain worldwide attention for the UNIA's proposed educational program.

Many of the leading figures in Jamaica's white society, including the colonial governor and the bishop of the Anglican church, encouraged Garvey's work, providing him with some financial support and attending UNIA social functions when invited. They were interested in his educational program, not his political views. Garvey, of course, was opposed to the whites' domination of the black population, and membership in his organization was restricted to people of his own race, but he favored racial cooperation in Jamaica. On the other hand, he believed that black society should remain separate from white society. "I want to have Jamaica a country of 'Black and White,' all living in peace and harmony but with equal rights and opportunities," he said. Such a policy, he knew, would eventually bring Jamaica's black majority into power.

Although Garvey received some support from prominent white liberals, Jamaica's colored middle class was openly hostile to the UNIA. The product of intermarriage between the races, the coloreds jealously guarded their position as intermediaries between blacks and whites. Although they were not allowed to hold any important offices in the government, the coloreds were usually wealthier and better educated than blacks. They considered themselves more white than black and superior to the common black laborer. Most of them felt threatened by Garvey's racial-solidarity movement.

The option of joining the colored class had been open to Garvey. Normally, educated blacks such as Garvey tried to improve their standing by marrying into the colored middle class. Those who did so were seeking to break their ties with fellow blacks—denying their "inferior" blood. Garvey could not make such a compromise, and he knew that by refusing to do so he was endangering some old friendships. "I had to decide whether to please my friends and be one of the 'black-whites' of Jamaica, and be reasonably prosperous, or come out openly and defend and help improve and protect the integrity of the black millions and suffer," Garvey wrote later. "I decided to do the latter."

Jamaica's colored leaders responded to Garvey's attempts to organize the blacks with scalding attacks on him in the local newspapers. "I was openly hated and persecuted by some of those colored men on the island, who did not want to be classified as Negroes, but as white," Garvey recalled. "They hated me worse than poison." He was bitterly disappointed about the treatment he received from the coloreds. These were the educated people he had hoped would be at the forefront of the crusade for black advancement. Instead, they had rejected their African heritage.

The coloreds' disdainful attitude toward their black ancestry produced an opposite reaction in Garvey. "When Europe was inhabited by a race of cannibals, a race of savages, naked men, heathens, and pagans, Africa was peopled with a race of cultured black men, who were masters in art, science and literature," Garvey taught the UNIA's members. The superiority of African to European civilization was to become a central point of his philosophy. He would continue to look back to an Africa inhabited by "men who were cultured and refined; men who, it was said, were like the gods."

By late 1915, however, Garvey was forced to recognize that his movement was struggling. The UNIA had attracted only about 100 members, and it was clear to the black population that the organization could do little to help them. Garvey admitted that he was finding his work "harassing and heartrending." Much of his talk about the glories of ancient Africa was probably lost on impoverished farmers struggling to feed their families. In addition, his colored opponents had used their considerable influence to discredit the UNIA. White sympathizers whom Garvey was counting on to help fund a Jamaican Tuskegee Institute were, after World War I began in 1914, preoccupied with the news coming from the European battlefronts.

IN HIS OWN WORDS...

Marcus Garvey began the UNIA in hopes of uniting the black population in an atmosphere of racial pride that promoted education and opportunity. He laid out the beliefs of the organization in an issue of *Negro World*, an official UNIA newspaper created by Garvey.

What We Believe

The Universal Negro Improvement Association advocates the unity and blending of all Negroes into a strong, healthy race.

It is against miscegenation [racial intermarriage] and race suicide.

It believes that the Negro race is as good as any other, and therefore should be as proud of itself as the others are.

It believes in the purity of the Negro race and the purity of the white race.

It is against rich blacks marrying poor whites.

It is against rich or poor whites taking advantage of Negro women.

It believes in the spiritual Fatherhood of God and the Brotherhood of Man.

Marcus Garvey, *Negro World*, 1924

Realizing that he would have to look elsewhere for the money to carry out his programs, Garvey decided to make a fund-raising tour of the southern United States. He wrote to Booker T. Washington about his plans, hoping that Tuskegee's director would introduce him to American audiences. In late 1915, Garvey learned that Washington had died. Saddened by the loss of the man he so admired, Garvey nonetheless continued to prepare for his trip. He did not care that he had no friends in America, for he believed it was his mission in life to lead his people. Wherever Garvey found members of his race living in oppression, he would also find followers.

4

"Up, You Mighty Race"

When the 28-year-old Garvey arrived in the United States on March 23, 1916, he found a large black population that was ready to listen to ideas about racial pride and self-improvement. American blacks were tired of being the victims of prejudice and mob violence in their own country and were seeking a leader who could restore their dignity and self-respect. Garvey believed he could be that leader.

Few people in 1916 had heard of the UNIA or its founder, and Garvey arrived in New York City without fanfare. He lodged with a Jamaican family in Harlem, an area that had recently become the center of the city's black population. A strong black community organization was well established, and the district had already gained a reputation as a place where blacks could come to pursue their own culture free from harassment. Among those who had flocked to Harlem was the ragtime pianist and composer Scott Joplin. The district also supported a thriving business community and a growing black protest movement.

During his first months in New York, Garvey worked as a printer and spent his free time on street corners, explaining his program for racial solidarity to anyone who would listen. The Harlem blacks regarded him curiously—this Jamaican who spoke so fervently about the wonders of Africa. Too short to have much of a presence in crowds, Garvey stood on boxes to give his speeches. Sometimes, weak from hunger, he fell off his stand. He caught many colds standing chilled and damp in his worn-out shoes and thin suits. Though he tried hard to win a following, Harlem was not ready for him. American blacks were more interested in racial problems in their own country than in the situation in faraway Africa.

After three months in New York, Garvey had saved enough money to begin his lecturing and fund-raising tour. As in Latin America and Europe, he traveled extensively, speaking in major cities from Boston to Washington, D.C., to Chicago and visiting nearly every state with a large black population. He spoke about conditions in Jamaica and the Caribbean and met with black community leaders to hear their views about the racial situation in the United States. During his travels Garvey learned about the history of black Americans and became familiar with the serious problems they faced throughout the country.

Since 1619, when the first group of African slaves had been brought to Virginia, blacks had toiled in the fields, shops, and homes of white Americans. The institution of slavery became firmly established throughout the South as Americans moved west, but it gradually died out in the North after the Revolutionary War. The slave trade with Africa was finally outlawed in 1808, but most blacks in the South remained in bondage until 1863. On January 1 of that year, midway through the American Civil War, President Abraham Lincoln issued the Emancipation Proclamation, which freed all slaves in the Confederate states.

BIG MASS MEETING

A CALL TO THE
COLORED CITIZENS
OF
ATLANTA, GEORGIA
To Hear the Great West Indian Negro Leader
HON. MARCUS GARVEY
President of the Universal Negro Improvement Association
of Jamaica, West Indies.

Big Bethel A. M. E. Church
Corner Auburn Avenue and Butler Street

SUNDAY AFTERNOON, AT 3 O'CLOCK
MARCH 25, 1917
He brings a message of inspiration to the
12,000,000 of our people in this country.
SUBJECT:
"The Negroes of the West Indies, after 78 years of Emancipation." With a general talk on the world position of the race.

An orator of exceptional force, Professor Garvey has spoken to packed audiences in England, New York, Boston, Washington, Philadelphia, Chicago, Milwaukee, St. Louis, Detroit, Cleveland, Cincinatti, Indianapolis, Louisville, Nashville and other cities. He has travelled to the principal countries of Europe, and was the first Negro to speak to the Veterans' Club of London, England.

This is the only chance to hear a great man who has taken his message before the world. COME OUT EARLY TO SECURE SEATS. It is worth travelling 1,000 miles to hear.

All Invited. Rev. R. H. Singleton, D.D., Pastor.

Though Garvey was mostly ignored when he came to the United States to promote his ideas on race and the UNIA, he soon improved his speaking skills and won supporters. This handbill advertises one of the mass meetings held by Garvey to discuss the issues of the black race around the world.

When the Civil War ended in 1865, blacks held great hopes for their future in the United States. From 1867 to 1877, the South underwent the process of Reconstruction, during which the formerly rebellious states were brought back into the Union. Congress passed laws that forced white Southerners to give equal rights to their ex-slaves. Black males were given the right to vote and to run for public office. In general, blacks expected an improvement in their economic and social status.

These hopes gradually faded in the following decades as the Southern state governments fell into the control of men opposed to black progress. Blacks remained primarily in the South. Most were poor, owned little land, and were denied opportunities for advancement that were open to whites. In the 1890s, Southern states began to pass laws denying voting privileges to anyone who could not meet certain literacy or property-ownership standards. The poor, mainly uneducated Southern blacks were stripped of their voting rights.

Although discrimination was worst in the South—where the so-called Jim Crow laws allowed whites to bar blacks from restaurants and hotels and to force them to attend separate schools—segregation was also common in the North. Race riots in New York City in 1900 and in Springfield, Illinois, in 1908 demonstrated that attacks on blacks by white mobs were possible anywhere in the country.

Shortly before Garvey arrived in the United States, black hopes for winning equal rights had revived. In 1914, World War I broke out in Europe. The United States remained neutral during the first years of the conflict, but American industries increased production to meet orders for supplies from the warring European nations. Northern factories had previously depended on recent immigrants from Europe to fill job openings in their plants, but wartime attacks on ships in the Atlantic reduced the flow of traffic from abroad. Companies began sending representatives to the South in search of cheap sources of labor. These agents promised jobs with good pay to any blacks who moved to the Northern cities to work. Many poor farmers leaped at the offer and moved their families north. There they hoped to find a better way of life.

body manures the earth, or to live God's purpose to the fullest?" He continued to complete his thought in that compelling, yet pleading voice for nearly an hour. I stood there like one in a trance, every sentence ringing in my ears, and finding an echo in my heart. When I walked out of that church, I was a different man . . . and so help me! I am still on the Garvey train.

Busy with UNIA organizational work, Garvey had little time to worry about his own income or comfort. His hard work paid off, and by the middle of 1919, he was claiming that the UNIA had attracted 2 million members in 30 chapters around the world. Although these figures are probably extreme exaggerations, they do reflect the widespread influence of the organization. "No one will ever know the accurate membership of the Universal Negro Improvement Association," declared Garvey, "because every second Negro you meet, if not an actual member, is one in spirit."

No matter what the true membership figures for the UNIA really were, it is clear that, by 1919, Garvey was finding recruiting easy in America's worsening racial climate. World War I ended in 1918, and the country's economic boom ended with it. The men who had gone overseas to fight after the United States entered the war in 1917 returned home looking for work. Immigrants from Europe again began to arrive in America. Blacks who had moved north for jobs and good wages found that they were the first to be fired once the labor shortage eased up. The competition for jobs, combined with the friction caused by the growth of black communities in Northern cities, bred increasing racial hostilities. By 1919, these tensions exploded into race riots in cities across the United States.

VIOLENCE, BLOOD, AND RACE

In Chicago, the drowning of a black boy who accidentally swam into the white section of a public beach touched off cries

Black soldiers, like this group leaving France after winning the croix de guerre bravery medal, were shocked to find increased racial violence and discrimination upon their return to the United States after World War I. Many blacks were outraged that their willingness to help their country during war was rewarded with increased oppression, and they turned to Garvey for solutions.

of murder and led to 13 days of bloody racial violence. Further rioting occurred in 1919 in such places as Washington, D.C., Longview, Texas, and Elaine, Arkansas. Some of the outbursts were sparked by rumors of black assaults on white women, others by white attacks on black homes and churches. Although blacks defended themselves, they invariably got the worst of the battles with white mobs and hostile police.

The increase in racial violence was accompanied by a revival of the Ku Klux Klan. Founded in 1866, this dreaded white supremacist organization had won a large following in the

South after the Civil War. The hooded and white-robed Klansmen launched terror attacks against blacks and fought to overturn the racial-equality measures passed during Reconstruction. The second Klan started in Georgia in 1915 and included Jews, Catholics, and foreigners among its targets. Blacks were the Klan's favorite victims, however, and many were kidnapped and lynched by white-robed mobs. Among those lynched were black soldiers returning home from the battlefields of World War I.

American blacks were shocked by the violence directed at them. They had supported the war effort enthusiastically, enlisting in the armed forces in great numbers and using their hard-earned savings to buy war bonds. Instead of greater freedom, however, blacks faced worse oppression after the war. Disillusioned about their chances for achieving equality in America, an increasing number of blacks were turning to Garvey for leadership.

The UNIA extended a welcoming hand to the restless black masses. As Garvey traveled around the country recruiting new members, he repeatedly emphasized the theme of universal black solidarity. "I know no national boundary where the Negro is concerned," he told his listeners, instructing them to reach out to their brothers and sisters in other countries. "Up, you mighty race" became the rallying cry of the UNIA.

In his speeches, Garvey continued to stress the importance of a good education. He told blacks to be proud of their race, for their African ancestors had been masters of the arts and sciences. White societies, he said, were "but duplicates of a grander civilization" created in Africa centuries before. He also told his audiences to look to people of their own race for models and to save their admiration for black heroes. They should put the interests of their race before those of their country.

Another of Garvey's proposals was that blacks stop worshiping a white God and pray to a divine being who was black. He admitted that God really had no skin color, but he was disturbed that many blacks hung pictures on the walls of their homes that showed God as a white man. This difference between themselves and the way they saw God could only make blacks think of themselves as members of an inferior race.

The KKK

The Ku Klux Klan leaders with whom Marcus Garvey met in 1922 represented an organization in its second incarnation that already was known across the country as America's most notorious racist group. Founded in Pulaski, Tennessee, in 1866 and led by prominent ex-Confederates such as Nathan Bedford Forrest, the "first" Klan concentrated its efforts on bringing down Republican governments and restricting black civil rights throughout the South. To achieve these ends, the Klan relied on violence and intimidation—so much so that it provoked uncharacteristically swift federal action. In 1871, the United States government moved aggressively to suppress the group, with the result that, within a year, the Klan essentially ceased to exist.

Like a weed, however, the organization sprang up again. It resurfaced in 1915, in Stone Mountain, Georgia, energized by widespread racist sentiment of the type found in Thomas Dixon's popular novel *The Clansman* (1905) and D.W. Griffith's blockbuster silent film *The Birth of a Nation* (1915). This "second" Klan started a reign of terror that left thousands of blacks and even some whites, mainly Roman Catholics and Jews, dead or injured across America. Claiming to be the sole defenders of the white race, the Klan rampaged from Oregon to Georgia and once had the audacity to march down Pennsylvania Avenue in Washington, D.C., flaunting their hate. By the mid-1920s, the Ku Klux Klan had more than three million white-hooded members coast to coast.

The Great Depression and World War II fixed popular attention on the economy at home and war overseas. As a result, by 1944, the Klan had withered and died once more.

The latest incarnation of the KKK rose to prominence during the civil rights battles of the 1950s and 1960s and persists today as small, locally based hate groups and racist publications and Web sites. Yet despite small numbers and loose organization, the Klan remains as dangerous as when Marcus Garvey ill advisedly chose to meet with its members.

"[Angels] are not white peaches from Georgia," he said. "We are going to make them beautiful black peaches from Africa."

For the same reason, Garvey told parents to give their children black dolls to play with. He cried out against the skin-bleaching and hair-straightening products that many blacks used to make themselves look "more white," and he forbade the *Negro World* to accept advertisements for such merchandise. "God made us as his perfect creation," he said. "He made no mistake when he made us black with kinky hair. . . . Now take those kinks out of your mind instead of your hair."

Garvey told his followers the things that blacks wanted to hear—that their race could rise up and be free, proud, and powerful. Others had said it before, but none with Garvey's passion. By 1919 his fame was beginning to spread around the globe. The UNIA had purchased a large auditorium in Harlem to serve as its headquarters. The building, renamed Liberty Hall, was filled nearly every night with thousands of adoring "Garveyites" straining to hear the voice of the prophet of black pride. Soon other UNIA branches were naming their meeting halls after the famous Harlem auditorium.

There were many people in the United States who did not look kindly on Garvey's movement. Most whites believed he was a dangerous anti-American fanatic who was inciting blacks to attack whites. Many black intellectuals thought his ideas were crude and simplistic. Some black clergymen supported him wholeheartedly, but others accused him of trying to steal their congregations from them. He engaged in long-running disputes with rival political leaders and the editors of other black newspapers. Finally, even some UNIA officials found him to be arrogant and unwilling to accept any criticism.

Garvey's task was immensely difficult, and he was bound to stir up much controversy no matter what he did. In October 1919 his life nearly came to an end. He was sitting in his New York office when a former employee named George Tyler stormed in and demanded that he be given $25 that he was owed. Suddenly, Tyler drew out a gun and fired several times. Garvey was lucky to escape serious injury, but one bullet grazed his forehead, and another struck his leg. His secretary, Amy Ashwood, grappled with the gunman and forced him to flee.

Tyler was apprehended later in the day but died under mysterious circumstances, supposedly jumping to death from the prison cell where he was being held. Before he died, Tyler had reportedly said that he had been sent to murder Garvey. No accomplices were ever found, however, and the police treated the matter as a private dispute between Garvey and Tyler.

Garvey soon recovered from his wounds, and his popularity soared. The black press trumpeted him as a hero of his race, a great leader who had almost been struck down while shielding his people from racial bigotry. For the moment his critics were silenced, and his followers were cheering on the man they called Black Moses.

5

Star of Destiny

Early in 1919, Garvey made an announcement that electrified the black community: The UNIA was founding a giant shipping company that would be owned and operated entirely by blacks. The new firm was christened the Black Star Line.

Advertisements were placed in the *Negro World* and other newspapers inviting blacks to buy stock in their own steamship line. Garvey's shipping venture opened whole new horizons to blacks. Millions were swept up by the vision of a fleet representing the entire race, proudly bearing the Black Star flag into all the world's ports.

The formation of the Black Star Line was Garvey's opening shot in his battle to achieve black economic independence. The maritime company was intended to be many times the size of any black-owned business then in existence. As he explained to his followers, "Our economic condition seems, to a great extent, to affect our general status. . . . Be not deceived, wealth is strength, wealth is power, wealth is justice, is liberty, is real human rights."

To Garvey, the Black Star Line was far more than a shipping company; it embodied within it the struggle for black rights. Because black employees and customers were discriminated against in the white-dominated business world, their only hope for winning economic security was to found and patronize their own stores and companies.

One tool for helping blacks start their own businesses was the Negro Factories Corporation, which was established by the UNIA in 1919. The goal of this association was, the *Negro World* announced, to "build and operate factories in the big industrial centers of the United States, Central America, the West Indies, and Africa to manufacture every marketable commodity." Stock in the corporation sold for $1 a share, and Garvey preached to the masses that by investing in the UNIA firm, blacks would be creating jobs for themselves and their children.

While never growing to the extent envisioned by the *Negro World*, the Negro Factories Corporation did start and operate many businesses in Harlem. These included a chain of grocery stores, laundries, restaurants, clothing stores, a doll factory, and a small publishing house. The corporation also supplied guidance and issued loans to black businesses.

The UNIA's most ambitious project was the Black Star Line. While Garvey's critics grudgingly praised his other economic projects, his proposals for a black shipping line met with great skepticism. The general black population had fewer doubts, however, and the $5-a-share company stock was sold almost as fast as it could be printed. In September 1919, Garvey announced that the line had made its first purchase, the 32-year-old merchant ship *Yarmouth*, for the impressive sum of $165,000.

Even before the Black Star Line was officially established, Garvey had told UNIA members that he was collecting money to buy ships. They responded enthusiastically, and more than $600,000 worth of stock was sold during the line's first year. UNIA supporters scraped together their savings to buy shares, and money poured in from all over the world. "I have sent twice to buy shares amounting to $125," wrote a stockholder from Panama. "Now I am sending $35 for seven more shares. You might think I have money, but the truth, as I stated before, is that I have no money now. But if I'm to die of hunger it will be all right because I'm determined to do all that's in my power to better the conditions of my race."

Buoyed by the initial success of the Black Star Line, Garvey began to make plans for a huge extravaganza that would display the UNIA's growing power. Late in 1919, he sent a message to UNIA branches and to other black organizations: A convention of delegates representing all the black peoples of the world would be held in New York during August 1920. The purpose of the convention was to organize the black race into a united front. Delegates would draw up a Negro Declaration of Rights and then present it to all the world's governments.

Garvey was also in the news for another reason. He and his secretary, Amy Ashwood, were married on December 25, 1919. A lavish wedding ceremony took place in Harlem's Liberty Hall. It was a taste of the festivities that would occur the following August. Details of Garvey's ambitious scheme circulated throughout Harlem, but they gave the black world little preparation for the magnificent spectacle he organized that summer. Delegates came from as far away as Africa and South America; packed convention sessions were held in Liberty Hall for 30 days. The 1920 First International Convention of the Negro Peoples of the World made both blacks and whites sit up and take notice of Garvey and his program.

A GRAND GATHERING

The convention opened on Sunday, August 1, with religious services and a silent march of delegates and UNIA members through Harlem. The next day, the true spectacle began. Garvey had organized a giant parade through the streets of Harlem. Much of the district closed down as thousands lined the streets to watch the procession. Garvey rode in an open car, wearing a fancy uniform and a plumed hat. He was not the only one dressed for the occasion. Spectators were astonished to view an army of UNIA groups.

First in line were members of the African Legions, some riding horses, some marching on foot. They were outfitted in blue uniforms with bright red trouser stripes. The group's members were unarmed and were used by Garvey mainly for ceremonial purposes, but their military bearing suggested the hidden power of the black race. Garvey hoped that the Legions could one day be used to reclaim Africa from its foreign occupiers.

Following the African Legions were 200 Black Cross nurses, marching in long white dresses and white stockings. Few of the nurses had any actual medical training, but they symbolized the UNIA's commitment to aiding sick and needy members of the black community. In the middle of the parade came the officers and crew of the Black Star Line, who received huge ovations from the crowd. After them marched the Women's Auxiliary, a female counterpart of the African Legions. Next came a group of proud young Garveyites, the UNIA Juveniles. At the end of the parade were several brass bands, the UNIA choir, and the thousands of convention delegates who had responded to Garvey's call.

The marchers carried banners that proclaimed "Down with Lynching," "Join the Fight for Freedom," and "Africa Must Be Free." Some of the women waved signs reading "God Give Us Real Men." Many of those watching felt for the first time the power and united spirit of an aroused black race.

On the night of August 2, people gathered at Madison Square Garden, the largest indoor auditorium in New York, to hear the words of their leader, Marcus Garvey. The crowd filled the hall of the auditorium and spilled out into the streets. Inside

**Encouraged by the success of his business ventures, Garvey
held the First Convention of the Negro Peoples of the World
in 1920. The event lasted 30 days, and featured speeches,
meetings, and a parade of various representatives from the
black community. Here, Garvey rides in the parade, dressed
in a military costume and plumed hat.**

the hall, the convention finally got under way. The people in
the audience sang the new UNIA anthem, "Ethiopia, Thou
Land of Our Fathers" (Ethiopia is an ancient name for Africa),
and were entertained by bands as they waited impatiently for
Garvey to appear.

Dressed in dark robes, Garvey finally stepped onto the stage and received a five-minute standing ovation. When the clapping died down, he made an announcement: The UNIA had sent a telegram to Eamon De Valera, the leader of the Irish independence movement, expressing the convention's support for Ireland's struggle to free itself from British rule. Ireland was in the process of winning self-rule, and De Valera had assumed the title of president of the Irish Republic. The UNIA telegram stated: "We believe Ireland should be free even as Africa shall be free for the Negroes of the world. Keep up the fight for a free Ireland." (For additional information this Irish leader, enter "Eamon De Valera" into any search engine and browse the sites listed.)

The telegram highlighted one of the main thrusts of Garvey's program: the need for an independent black-ruled nation in Africa. He had long sympathized with the Irish cause, and by comparing that struggle to the black desire for self-rule in Africa, he drew international attention to his own campaign. All oppressed people were tied together, he said. "We are the descendants of a suffering people, we are the descendants of a people determined to suffer no longer."

IN HIS OWN WORDS...

Marcus Garvey believed Africa was the only place where black people could truly have freedom and equality with other races. In Africa, the black man was in the majority, and by becoming powerful there he could gain power around the world. Garvey discusses this opinion in a 1929 article from his Jamaican newspapers *The Blackman*:

> We are determined to solve our own problem by redeeming our Motherland Africa from the hands of alien exploiters and found there a Government, a nation of our own, strong enough to lend protection to the members of our race scattered all over the world, and to compel the respect of the nations and races of the earth.

In his speeches at the convention, Garvey stressed that Africa belonged to the black peoples of the world. He warned the European colonial powers that blacks were "coming 400 million strong, and we mean to retake every square inch of the 12 million square miles of African territory belonging to us by right Divine." The statement was backed by Garvey's slogan "Let Africa be our guiding star—Our Star of Destiny."

Garvey was just beginning to form his ambitious plans for a black homeland. Eventually, he believed, Africa would become a magnet for all blacks in search of a nation that would allow them full rights as citizens. The convention raised hopes that this vision could become a reality.

For four weeks the speeches and meetings continued. In the midst of all this commotion, the UNIA was raising lots of money for its various operations. Stock in the Black Star Line and the Negro Factories Corporation was purchased in massive quantities. People who contributed sums of $50 or more to the UNIA were given special bronze, silver, or gold crosses known as African Redemption medals.

Acting as representatives of the worldwide black community, the delegates set up a model government for a future black nation. They elected Garvey provisional president of Africa, the head of a government in exile. Leading UNIA officials received titles such as "knight of the Nile." The delegates chose a flag of red, black, and green to represent the new UNIA-sponsored nation: red for the blood shed by blacks to make themselves free, black for their skin color, and green for the lush African forests. All of this was done to demonstrate to blacks that they were capable of creating institutions that equaled those of whites.

The convention's most important task was the composition of the Declaration of Rights of the Negro Peoples of the World. In order to prepare a document that would truly represent blacks throughout the world, the writers of the declaration listened to delegates report on the conditions in their countries.

The Black Cross Nurses, who symbolized the UNIA's commitment to sick and poor black community members, were one of many groups to march in Garvey's 1920 convention. The convention instilled feelings of pride and unity in the black people who attended it, and Garvey hoped it would lead to important changes in the position of the black race in the world.

The first section of the declaration protested that blacks were "denied the common rights due to human beings for no other reason than their race and color." The document condemned all forms of discrimination, lynching, unequal school systems for blacks, and the denial of equal pay for equal work.

Following the declaration's section on black grievances came a list of 54 rights that all countries should give to their Negro citizens. The convention stated that blacks should be accorded the right to participate in politics and should receive the same legal rights as other citizens. "Negro" should be written with a capital N, the declaration pointed out. Africans should be given their freedom. Lastly, the declaration proclaimed that August 31, the final day of the convention, was to be an annual international holiday for blacks.

This was a declaration to make blacks proud, and it made everyone take notice of the great movement that was stirring within the Negro race. "The nations of the world are aware that the Negro of yesterday has disappeared from the scene of human activities," Garvey declared after the convention. "His place has been taken by a new Negro who stands erect, conscious of his manhood rights and fully determined to preserve them at all costs."

6

Proud Ships
Sailing in Circles

When Garvey started his new shipping venture in 1919, he promised that the Black Star Line would make large profits for its investors. This opportunity to make money was of secondary concern to many of the firm's stockholders. Far more important to them was that the Black Star Line gave them a tremendous feeling of hope about the future of their race. The cheering crowds that greeted the ships in every port they visited were filled with a newfound sense of pride when they saw the vessels flying the red, black, and green UNIA flag.

While the multitudes cheered, however, some of Garvey's critics were asking a troublesome question: Did Garvey or any of his UNIA associates know anything about running a steamship line? The answer was no. The Black Star Line's board of managers had little business experience, and some of the line's officials were more intent on lining their own pockets than on operating a profitable shipping company.

Garvey gave little thought as to what kind of ships he needed, how they should be maintained, what cargo they would carry, or where they would sail. He looked upon the ships as promotional tools that would be used to spread the UNIA's message. After purchasing the Black Star Line's flagship, the *Yarmouth*, Garvey announced that the vessel was being renamed the *Frederick Douglass* after the leading black spokesman of the antislavery movement in pre-Civil War America. (The ship remained officially known as the *Yarmouth* because the Black Star Line, for financial reasons, failed to register it under its new name.) Garvey immediately scheduled a voyage to the West Indies and hired one of the only qualified black captains, Joshua Cockbourne, to command the ship. On October 31, thousands of Garveyites gathered at New York's 135th Street pier to see the *Yarmouth* off.

The grand bon voyage almost turned into a humiliating fiasco. Just before the scheduled departure, a representative of the *Yarmouth*'s previous owners appeared with an order forbidding the ship to sail until it was fully insured. Garvey had only made a down payment on the ship, and the previous owner was nervous about the voyage. With the excited crowd waiting nearby, however, the agent relented. The ship was allowed to sail, but only as far as the 23rd Street pier. There the ship remained until Garvey obtained the insurance. The *Yarmouth* finally departed from New York, but the initial delay was a sign of the troubles that the ship and the Black Star Line would undergo.

The *Yarmouth* was hardly in tip-top shape. Its boilers were old and in need of repair, and the ship could rarely work up any speed. "The *Yarmouth* was not a vessel to set a sailor's heart aflame," wrote Hugh Mulzac, an officer on the ship. He estimated that the vessel was worth less than one sixth what the Black Star line paid for it. Financially, the first voyage was a total loss. The *Yarmouth* sailed from New York nearly empty, and it carried few passengers and little cargo on its return trip.

Garvey, here in 1921, hit frequent roadblocks with his projects that were intended to give blacks equality, opportunity, and hope. His biggest venture, the Black Star Line, was a financial failure, and Garvey was eventually arrested on accusations of mail fraud associated with the shipping line.

The ship was greeted by large crowds in every port it visited, and sales of company stock soared—but operating the ship was a huge financial drain.

The *Yarmouth*'s second voyage was no better than the first. Cockbourne dumped half the ship's cargo of whiskey overboard, supposedly to lighten the ship after it started to list. A fleet of boats was waiting by the ship to salvage the jettisoned cargo, so the captain's actions seemed suspicious. The ship spent its second voyage ferrying between ports in the Caribbean, losing money on each trip. Many stops were made merely to promote Black Star Line stock. On the *Yarmouth*'s return to the United States, Cockbourne ran the ship aground in Boston, and Garvey fired him.

The *Yarmouth* made one more unprofitable voyage and then was sold in late 1921 for a paltry $1,625. Neither of the Black Star Line's other two ships fared any better. In early 1920, Garvey purchased the *Shadyside*, a small 50-year-old excursion boat, for $35,000. The vessel was used for Hudson River pleasure cruises and catered to Harlemites who wanted to get away from the city on hot summer days—but the ancient *Shadyside* was costly to operate, and Garvey was forced to retire the ship after less than a year of service. The boat finally sank during a winter storm while tied up at its dock. The company's other ill-fated ship was the *Kanawha*, an old pleasure yacht that was purchased for $60,000 in 1920. The ship could only carry a small cargo and, like the *Yarmouth*, was used mainly to advertise the shipping line and raise money for the UNIA. After a series of engine failures that required expensive repairs, Garvey ordered that the ship be abandoned in Cuba.

TRYING TO SALVAGE THE BLACK STAR WRECK

As early as November 1919, Garvey had promised that the Black Star Line would acquire a ship capable of sailing to African ports. By October 1920, the expenses of buying and operating the *Yarmouth*, *Shadyside*, and *Kanawha* had crippled the Black Star Line. To get around these difficulties, Garvey formed another enterprise, the Black Star Steamship Company of New Jersey, which could raise money for another vessel free of any legal connection to the financially troubled Black Star Line.

The new corporation's stock sold well, and Garvey began seeking a satisfactory ship, which he intended to name the *Phillis Wheatley* after the first black American poet. Several attempts were made to purchase such a vessel, but all ended in failure. By the end of 1921, Black Star shipping operations had nearly ceased.

While the Black Star Line had been sailing into troubled waters, Garvey had also been pursuing other parts of his program. Chief among these were his efforts to secure an independent African homeland for all of the world's blacks. Many people believed that Garvey was intending to lead all blacks living outside of Africa in a return to the great continent. The UNIA therefore became known as a "Back-to-Africa" movement. According to some of Garvey's close associates, he never envisioned a sudden mass emigration to Africa. He proposed only that a few thousand American blacks move to Africa and establish an independent nation committed to fighting for the rights of blacks everywhere. He did hope, however, that the initial groups would be followed by much larger emigrations over time.

Garvey feared for blacks living in countries where they were a minority. He believed that continual demands for equality by American blacks would threaten whites and lead to increasingly violent racial conflicts. A strong African nation, however, might be able to force other countries to respect the rights of their black citizens.

Some of Garvey's impoverished working-class followers were swept up in the dream of escaping their troubles through the "Back-to-Africa" movement. His critics charged that his ideas were hopelessly unrealistic. Black Americans, they said, must forget about moving to Africa, where they were total strangers, and concentrate on improving conditions in the United States. How could black Americans go back to a place where they had never been?

"Back to Africa"

One of Marcus Garvey's favorite sayings reveals his truly universal perspective when it came to racial dignity: "A strong man is strong everywhere." Distilled, this particular aphorism (statement of a principle) implies that black self-determination could not be achieved in one place without existing in every other. For Garvey, Africa represented a hub for a worldwide movement. Within this context, Garvey's particular definition of the term "back to Africa" differed substantially from the one that had emerged a century earlier.

Garvey was not the first to envision blacks returning to Africa; indeed, his only innovation lay in the fact that he envisioned such a migration as a prerequisite for the founding of a powerful black nation on the continent. Garvey imagined that this new "mother country" would draw on the creative energies of black men and women from around the world and would base itself on an economy driven by the exploitation of abundant natural resources. As this state grew in power and prosperity, it would protect and promote black interests globally. Thus, any exodus of African Americans stood less for a return to an ancestral homeland than as a tentative step toward a genuinely universal pan-African center of gravity.

This was something entirely new. Until the unveiling of the UNIA program, the phrase "back to Africa" had carried a radically different meaning. The idea of black Americans returning to Africa had been around, in some form, since the early nineteenth century. As early as 1817, with the formation of the American Colonization Society, white Americans had begun trying to erase the black presence in the young republic. Supporters of the Society's repatriation plan included two presidents—James Madison and James Monroe—one Supreme Court chief justice, and the famous American orator Daniel Webster. Whereas Garvey sought a return to Africa in the hope of empowering blacks, the ACS wanted to isolate them in a land its members and supporters labeled as forsaken. The ACS held long meetings on the subject of sending blacks back to their "home," and, in the end, the organization did far more than just talk. The Society purchased a large tract of land in West Africa in 1821 and immediately began transporting freed slaves across the Atlantic Ocean. Eventually, an estimated 12,000 African Americans arrived in what became the modern nation of Liberia. Marcus Garvey might have been the last person to argue seriously for a move "back to Africa," but he certainly was not the first.

Garvey made several attempts to realize his dream of an African homeland. After World War I, the defeated Germans were stripped of their African possessions. In 1922, Garvey sent a delegation to the League of Nations, the predecessor of the United Nations, to ask that the former German colonies be turned over to the UNIA. The league briefly considered the petition, but the matter was later dropped.

Knowing that his chance of gaining a colony through the League of Nations was a long shot, Garvey had previously opened negotiations with the West African nation of Liberia over the possibility of establishing settlements of black Americans there. Liberia had been founded in 1822 as a home for free black Americans who wanted to return to Africa, and Garvey assumed that the Liberian government would welcome the UNIA settlers. At first the Liberians did indeed seem open to the idea, and Garvey promised that his organization would build colleges, factories, and railroads in the African nation. The UNIA sent a small team to make arrangements for the new settlements. The expedition soon ran out of money, however, and Garvey was too involved in other matters to follow through on his plans. By early 1924, Garvey was ready to make another try. This time a UNIA delegation convinced Liberia to accept an initial settlement of a few thousand Americans. By the summer of 1924, however, when UNIA officials arrived to make final arrangements, the Liberian president Charles D.B. King's government had changed its position entirely. The delegation was told to go home; no settlements would be permitted.

Garvey desperately appealed to the Liberians to reconsider their decision, but to no avail. King clearly had begun to suspect that the UNIA was planning to overthrow his government once it had established a strong presence in his country. The Liberians were also afraid that France or Britain might invade their nation if UNIA agitators began to stir up trouble in the surrounding colonial areas. Finally, the land that the

UNIA had been promised was leased to the Firestone Rubber Company soon after the deal fell through.

The setback in Liberia occurred three years after the beginning of a series of events that was to isolate Garvey from much of the black community and devastate the UNIA. In the spring of 1921, Garvey toured throughout the West Indies and Central America selling Black Star Line stock. Although he raised considerable amounts of money, Garvey had a difficult time reentering the United States. The State Department declared him a dangerous radical and ordered the American consulates in the countries he was visiting to refuse to grant him a visa. The order was later rescinded, but Garvey was beginning to feel strong pressure from the U.S. government. Aware that he could easily be deported from the country by hostile government officials, he applied for U.S. citizenship.

On his return to New York, Garvey learned that his wife, Amy Ashwood Garvey, was suing for a legal separation on the grounds that he was having an affair with his new secretary, a Jamaican woman named Amy Jacques. The marriage had been troubled from the start, and Garvey had previously filed a divorce suit against his wife, which he later dropped. The Garveys' marital problems were widely discussed in the newspapers.

The second UNIA convention in August 1921 showed further evidence of an organization in trouble. Although the convention was well attended, some UNIA members demanded to see a report on the financial status of the Black Star Line. The feeling of black unity that marked the first convention was already beginning to wane.

After the convention, Garvey's long-cherished desire for a black church was finally realized. Acting at Garvey's request, an ex-chaplain of UNIA, George Alexander McGuire, formed the African Orthodox Church. In a ceremony held on September 28, 1921, McGuire was ordained as bishop of the church, which taught its members that God and Christ were black. Many religious leaders attacked the new church, but it won a wide following, claiming a membership of 250,000 at its peak. The church, however, served a broader purpose than spiritual uplift. The AOC was meant to spread the Garvey message throughout the black religious community.

By the end of 1921, the Black Star Line's financial problems were beginning to catch up to Garvey. His critics demanded to know what had become of the three quarters of a million dollars that investors had sunk in his shipping line. The postal

African Orthodox Church

While Marcus Garvey languished in an American prison, petitioners begged President Calvin Coolidge to release the man they considered their savior. One group from Panama went so far as to claim that, to them, Garvey was "a superman; a demigod; and the reincarnated Angel of Peace come from Heaven to dispense Political Salvation." Another band of supporters spoke of Garvey as part of the Holy Trinity: "God, the Creator of all things and people, His Son, the Spiritual Savior of all mankind . . . [and] Marcus Garvey, the leader of the Negro peoples of the world." Such bold, almost absurd declarations of Garvey's near divinity become understandable in the context of the leader's sincere, if rather eccentric, religiosity.

The head of UNIA felt sure that the God of peace and justice stood behind him and his movement. More important, this God was a black God, and a black God required a black church. The logical outgrowth of this conviction was a close affiliation between UNIA and the African Orthodox Church. Founded in 1921 by George Alexander McGuire, a former UNIA chaplain, the AOC became the de facto religious wing of Garvey's organization. Through the church and its official publication, the *Negro Churchman*, Garvey's message reached an audience that otherwise would have been unreceptive to his political and social ideas.

The AOC also extended UNIA's global reach. Congregations of the church sprang up from Canada to South Africa. Binding itself so closely to Garvey and UNIA, however, also guaranteed that the AOC's demise would coincide with that of its patron. The partnership between black religion and black politics was for the most part suspended on UNIA's disintegration, but it was not dissolved. Other men such as Martin Luther King, Jr., and Malcolm X would eventually reestablish it at another time with other agendas.

department charged that Garvey was circulating false advertisements in order to raise money for the Black Star Line. In January 1922, Garvey was arrested on a charge of using the mail to deceive Black Star Line investors. In February, he and three other company officials—Orlando Thompson, Elie Garcia, and George Tobias—were indicted on 12 counts of mail fraud. The four men were released on bail while the federal government conducted a thorough investigation into the operations of the Black Star Line. The trial would not begin until 15 months after the indictment was handed down. It was the beginning of the end for Garvey and his movement. His great business, the Black Star Line, was to be his downfall.

7

The Most Dangerous Enemy

As Garvey began his trial on March 21, 1923, he was aware that he was in deep trouble. His phenomenal success in building up the biggest black organization in history, his radical ideas, and his abrasive style had earned him the hatred of many enemies. The efforts of these foes, combined with the failings of his own organization, brought about the UNIA leader's ruin.

The most powerful force opposing Garvey was the U.S. government. Agents of the Justice Department had been watching his movements ever since his arrival in the United States. State Department officials periodically reported on UNIA activities in other countries. The UNIA was often described as dangerous in government reports on radical organizations. As early as 1919, FBI Director J. Edgar Hoover suggested in a memo that the government stifle Garvey by bringing fraud charges against him in connection with his Black Star Line business dealings. (For additional information on the FBI and its interest in Garvey, enter "J. Edgar Hoover and Garvey" into any search engine and browse the sites listed.)

Garvey's statements that blacks should put the interests of their race above those of their country were seen by government officials as a threat to law and order. He was accused of being unpatriotic for saying, shortly after the end of World War I, "The first dying that is to be done by the black man in the future will be done to make himself free . . . as for me, I think I have stopped dying for [the white man]." In 1921, when he was applying for U.S. citizenship, Garvey toned down his statements—but he remained firmly committed to the black separatist movement in America.

The U.S. government was not alone in wanting to silence Garvey. The European colonial powers saw the UNIA's strong backing for native self-rule movements as a threat to their control of Africa and other regions. They blamed Garvey for inciting race riots and workers' strikes in the colonies and barred him from entering many of their possessions.

Garvey made a number of enemies within his own race as well. The leaders of other black organizations resented Garvey's criticisms of their efforts to win a place for blacks within the larger white society. The most powerful of Garvey's opponents was W.E.B. Du Bois, renowned editor and writer, cofounder of the National Association for the Advancement of Colored People (NAACP), and tireless worker for racial cooperation.

Du Bois and his journal, the NAACP *Crisis*, had at first been mildly supportive of Garvey, calling him a "sincere, hardworking idealist." In late 1920, Du Bois wrote articles criticizing Garvey's management of the Black Star Line, but heated exchanges between the two did not really begin until the middle of 1922.

Du Bois published a series of damaging critiques of Garvey and his program and described the UNIA president as a "little, fat black man, ugly, but with intelligent eyes and a big head." For his part, Garvey mocked Du Bois for his light-colored

Garvey's often controversial projects and statements drew suspicion from the U.S. government and even from some members of his own race. W.E.B. Du Bois, cofounder of the NAACP, was one such black enemy of Garvey. Du Bois, seen here, supported integration, as opposed to the separatism espoused by Garvey, and the two men frequently attacked each other verbally.

skin and accused the NAACP leader of wishing that he were white. Ever since his disputes with Jamaica's colored population, Garvey had been hostile to lighter-skinned black leaders, believing that they looked down upon their darker brothers and sisters. Garvey mistrusted whites and excluded them from the UNIA. Du Bois's organization was open to both blacks and whites. Garvey believed that this was a dangerous mistake, for he felt that though "there may be a few good white men in America, there is no white man honest enough, sympathetic enough, humane enough, liberal enough to really take up the Negro's cause and fight it to a successful conclusion."

Garvey also criticized the NAACP's program of racial integration. The UNIA advocated racial separatism, believing that blacks and whites must establish their own separate social and political institutions—their own churches, their own schools, their own businesses, their own governments. The NAACP, Garvey charged, wanted to destroy the black race through intermarriage with whites. Du Bois and his kind, Garvey claimed, "believe that the black race will become, through social contact and intercourse, so mixed up with the white race as to produce a new type, probably like Du Bois himself, which will in time be the real American." Maintaining a "separate but equal" arrangement, in this case, translated into a vibrant, pure black race that could confront and compete with whites on their own terms. Garvey argued for a parallel global power structure in which distinct races checked and balanced one another in the pursuit of self-interested advancement.

THE STORM BREAKS

Many of Garvey's views were shared by the Ku Klux Klan and other white supremacist groups, who also believed in racial separatism and purity. Early in 1922, Garvey made a terrible mistake. Hoping to win Klan support for his Back to Africa movement, Garvey met with Klan leader Edward Young Clarke in Atlanta. Clarke wanted to learn about Garvey's views on racial purity and his plans for the black race. "I was speaking to a man who was brutally a white man, and I was speaking to him as a man who was brutally a Negro," Garvey said of the meeting. The two men were able to agree on many points. Clarke reportedly assured Garvey that the Klan would not interfere with UNIA activities.

Garvey obviously never supported the Klan's campaign of violence and terror against blacks, but he did believed that the Klan represented the true feelings of most white Americans toward blacks. He thought that the organized hostility of white supremacist groups was useful because it forced blacks to unite. He was also convinced that the Klan was too strong to fight and that blacks must seek their future in a free Africa. Yet, in the end, what linked Garvey to the Klan was a shared sense that blacks and whites simply could not, and more to the point should not, live together. True, the KKK took pride in its announced hatred of blacks, but Garvey had no love for whites either. Each race, he believed, must make its own way in the world. The black and white futures were distinct and incompatible.

Yet the majority of black American leaders vehemently disagreed. They joined in condemning Garvey for meeting with the Klan, and ultimately branded him as the worst kind of race traitor. Du Bois wrote, "Marcus Garvey is, without doubt, the most dangerous enemy of the Negro race in America

IN HIS OWN WORDS...

Marcus Garvey shared the belief of the Ku Klux Klan that blacks and whites were incompatible and should be separate, and he met with Klan leader Edward Young Clarke to discuss race issues. In his book *The Philosophy and Opinions of Marcus Garvey*, he discussed his opinions on the Klan:

> Between the Ku Klux Klan and the [NAACP], give me the Klan for their honesty and purpose towards the Negro. They are better friends to my race for telling us what they are, and what they mean, thereby giving us a chance to stir for ourselves, than all the hypocrites put together . . .

and in the world. He is either a lunatic or a traitor." William Pickens, a noted black educator, told Garvey, "You compare the aim of the Ku Klux Klan in America with your aim in Africa— and if that be true, no civilized man can endorse either of you." Garvey's critics were appalled that he was willing to give up the fight for black rights in America.

Further controversies dogged Garvey. On June 15, 1922, he divorced his wife, from whom he was separated, while she was away in England. A month later, he married his secretary, Amy Jacques. On her return to the United States, Amy Ashwood Garvey contested the divorce and Garvey's second marriage, but the suit failed. The black press, by now generally hostile to Garvey, supported the charges of misconduct filed against him by his ex-wife.

Hostility toward Garvey continued to grow. In August 1922, as delegates gathered for the third UNIA convention, a group opposed to Garvey, called the Friends of Negro Freedom, met in New York to denounce his alleged alliance with the Ku Klux Klan. Amid street fights between UNIA militants and their opponents, the cry of "Garvey must go" was heard loudly and clearly.

On January 15, 1923, eight leaders of the black community sent a letter to U.S. Attorney General Harry M. Daugherty asking the government to push ahead with its efforts to bring Garvey to trial. The case had been delayed for nearly a year while the government investigated the Black Star Line. The letter claimed that Garvey was trying to stir racial hatred and that his organization was involved in many acts of lawlessness and violence. Garvey lashed back at his attackers, accusing them of treachery to their race.

Whether or not the letter had any effect, four months later the trial began. Marcus Garvey, Elie Garcia, George Tobias, and Orlando Thompson were brought to trial for illegally sending false and misleading Black Star Line advertisements through the mail. The UNIA membership remained devoted to their

DID YOU KNOW?

Marcus Garvey's momentary flirtation with the Ku Klux Klan was not his last trip down the dark corridors of racial nationalism. The rise of Fascism in Italy and National Socialism (Nazism) in Germany attracted Garvey's attention and admiration very early on. Surveying the totalitarian landscapes being crafted by Benito Mussolini and Adolf Hitler, Garvey first regarded them with jealousy, wanting that success for his own efforts; later, he beamed with praise. Indeed, UNIA's founder ultimately revealed a distressing naïveté in his inability to recognize Mussolini and Hitler for the men they were. Garvey completely misread the objectives of the Fascist and Nazi programs and shamed himself by identifying black interests with men who eventually caused immeasurable suffering in Europe and Africa.

By the 1930s, Hitler already was laying the foundation for his war of racial genocide; at the same time, Mussolini was preparing to reestablish the Italian presence in Africa. Despite the obvious threats each man posed, Garvey construed their movements as akin to his own. He was neither blind to Hitler's overt racism nor oblivious to Mussolini's imperial pretensions, but he nonetheless lauded both dictators. In 1933, for example, Garvey declared that "Hitler, the German chancellor, cannot be mistaken for anything else than a patriot . . . Hitler stands for a greater Germany, which is his right, and the Negro should stand for a greater Africa which is also his right." Garvey similarly admired Italy's master but painted him as a Johnny-come-lately. Swelling with pride in 1937, Garvey told an audience that "UNIA was before Mussolini and Hitler were heard of. Mussolini and Hitler copied the program of UNIA . . . ." Two years earlier, Garvey had reminded an interviewer that people had "laughed at me because I dressed my followers up in uniforms and paraded them through the streets. But look at what Mussolini and Hitler have done with shirts and uniforms." Of the many follies and foibles that plagued and eventually destroyed Garvey and his movement, none proved as distasteful as his high regard for two tyrants who plunged the world into war and caused the deaths of millions of innocent people.

troubled leader. Thousands of letters and petitions objecting to the charges against him poured into government offices. During the trial, hundreds of supporters gathered around the courthouse, praying, protesting, and sometimes threatening the witnesses who testified against Garvey.

Garvey was convinced that government officials were intent on discrediting him and destroying his organization. Once the trial proceedings began, he became even more certain that he was caught in a trap. The judge, Julian Mack, was a contributor to the NAACP, the organization that Garvey considered his bitterest enemy. Garvey requested that Mack disqualify himself on the grounds that the judge might be unconsciously swayed to make rulings in favor of the prosecution. Mack refused, denying that he was biased in any way against the defendants.

Garvey hired one of the ablest black lawyers in America, Cornelius W. McDougald, for his defense. At the end of the first day of the trial, however, he dismissed McDougald. Always suspicious, Garvey believed that the lawyer was being used in the plot against him. For a while thereafter, Garvey conducted his own defense. His inexperience as a lawyer hurt his case. He showed off, made irrelevant speeches, argued continually with the judge's rulings, and generally prolonged the trial. He finally realized he needed help and accepted the services of a white lawyer named Armin Kohn.

The trial lasted for more than a month. The prosecution called 30 witnesses, many of them former Black Star Line employees and stockholders. The company's records were introduced as evidence. They revealed that the Black Star Line had been badly mismanaged. The charge that Garvey was personally dishonest was more difficult to prove. The government's case rested on the claim that Garvey mailed misleading advertisements to blacks to convince them to purchase Black Star Line stock. Although Garvey knew that his company was failing, the government claimed, he continued to send out advertisements that promised huge profits and dividends.

The main witness was Benny Dancy, a man who allegedly bought stock after receiving a Black Star Line advertisement. When questioned on the stand, however, Dancy displayed only a vague memory of what kind of mail he had been sent. He could not remember any specific details about the Black Star Line advertisement.

In his closing address to the jury, Garvey pointed out that the government had not proved that he had made any statements about his shipping company that he had known were false. He and the other defendants had only the best intentions regarding the Black Star Line, he added. "We had no monetary considerations or reward before us, but the good we could do for our race. . . . You will say it was bad business. But, gentlemen, there is something spiritual beside business. I ask no mercy. I ask no sympathy. I ask but for justice."

Garvey's entreaties were in vain. After deliberating for six hours, the jury found the Black Star Line president guilty of fraud. The other three defendants were acquitted. Garvey was flabbergasted. The trial, he angrily protested, was "a conspiracy to ruin Marcus Garvey. . . . I am satisfied to let the world judge me innocent or guilty. History will decide."

On June 21, 1923, Judge Mack sentenced Garvey to pay a $1,000 fine and to serve a five-year term in prison, the maximum sentence. UNIA lawyers immediately filed an appeal, and Garvey waited impatiently in the Tombs prison, a Manhattan detention center, while his organization tried desperately to raise the $15,000 bail. "My work is just begun," he wrote in prison, "and as I lay down my life for the cause of my people, so do I feel that succeeding generations shall be inspired by the sacrifice that I made for the rehabilitation of our race."

Garvey was finally released on bail three months later, and the ecstatic UNIA membership flocked to Liberty Hall to celebrate. He was convicted, Garvey told the crowd, "because I represented, even as I do now, a movement for the real

Garvey was put on trial for using the mail to send false advertisements regarding the Black Star Line. Though it was clear that the Black Star Line was badly mismanaged, there was no definitive evidence that Garvey had intentionally done anything wrong. Nevertheless, Garvey, seen here on his way to jail, was found guilty of fraud and sentenced to five years in prison.

emancipation of my race." Never one to take a temporary setback for defeat, he set out to rejuvenate his organization while his appeals dragged on in court. The first step was a new shipping line, and on March 20, 1924, he announced that he was forming the Black Cross Navigation and Trading Company.

The sorry fate of the Black Star Line had not weakened his followers' trust in him, and stock sales for the new company boomed. The line soon purchased the steamship *General G.W. Goethals* for $100,000 and scheduled a trip to the West Indies, departing from New York in January 1925. Unfortunately, the fate of the Black Cross vessel was depressingly similar to that of the Black Star Line ships. As usual, Garvey tried to finance the voyage by using the ship to sell stock along the way, and the *General G.W. Goethals* was forced to stop in port after port while attempts were made to raise enough money to continue. The ship was later sold to cover UNIA debts.

On February 2, 1925, Garvey's appeal was rejected. He was in Detroit on UNIA business and immediately returned to New York to surrender to the federal marshals. They handcuffed and arrested him as the train pulled into the station. On February 8, he was assigned to the Atlanta Federal Penitentiary, far from the center of UNIA activity in New York. In March, the U.S. Supreme Court rejected a final appeal by Garvey's lawyers to review his case.

Beginning his five-year term, Garvey wrote to his followers, "If I die in Atlanta my work shall only then begin, but I shall live, in the physical or spiritual [sense] to see the day of Africa's glory. With God's dearest blessings, I leave you for a while."

8

"Look for Me in the Whirlwind"

Behind bars in Atlanta, the once-powerful UNIA leader was assigned to work in the prison library. Garvey spent much of his time writing poetry, in which he expressed his frustration with the legal system that had convicted him. In his poem "The Tragedy of White Injustice," he wrote:

> Every man on his own foothold should stand,
> Claiming a nation and a fatherland!
> White, Yellow, and Black should make their own laws
> And force no one-sided justice with flaws.

Desperate to return to his work, Garvey wrote to President Calvin Coolidge three times requesting a pardon. These pleas went unanswered, so Garvey tried to conduct UNIA business from his cell. He continued to appoint the association's officers and to advise his New York headquarters on important matters. Amy Jacques Garvey worked heroically to hold the organization together, traveling to UNIA meetings throughout the country to speak in her husband's place. In 1925, she arranged for the publication of *Philosophy and Opinions of Marcus Garvey or Africa for the Africans*, an exhaustive collection of the UNIA leader's writings.

Garvey was not forgotten. Much of the black community was convinced that he had been unfairly treated. Former enemies forgave him and joined in his defense. His personal misfortunes seemed to prove his claim that blacks could not get a fair deal in the United States. UNIA members flooded government offices with letters, telegrams, and petitions demanding their leader's release. Rallies were held in many cities, and in the summer of 1926 a protest march in Harlem attracted more than 100,000 people.

The U.S. government took notice of the public clamor. "The situation as presented in the Garvey case is most unusual," Attorney General John Sargent wrote to President Coolidge in 1927. "Notwithstanding the fact that the prosecution was designated for the protection of colored people . . . none of those people apparently believe that they have been defrauded." Sargent stated that Garvey had regained his popularity and that his imprisonment was being seen as an attack on his race.

In response to pressure from the black community, Coolidge commuted Garvey's sentence and ordered his release on November 18, 1927. The 40-year-old UNIA leader had served more than half of his five-year sentence.

Garvey's troubles were not over. A decision on the application for U.S. citizenship that he had filed in 1921 had been delayed because of his legal troubles. Soon after entering prison in Atlanta, he learned that his petition for citizenship had been denied. Released from jail, he was still not a free man. The U.S. government declared that as a convicted criminal, the Jamaican troublemaker should be deported from the country.

The black community protested Garvey's incarceration, and President Calvin Coolidge responded by commuting Garvey's sentence and ordering his release in 1927, after he spent almost three years in jail. However, as a convicted criminal without U.S. citizenship, Garvey was deported to Jamaica. Here, in 1936, Garvey prepares to sail to London, where he moved his UNIA headquarters after his deportation.

Garvey was not even allowed to return to his New York head-quarters to say good-bye to his loyal membership. He was taken directly from Atlanta to New Orleans and put on board the *Saramacca*, a ship that was sailing to Panama. Guarded closely by federal officers, the UNIA president watched from the deck of the ship as hundreds of loyal Garveyites gathered at the docks to see him off. Garvey called out to his followers, "The UNIA is not something I have joined, it is something I have founded. I have set everything aside to do this work. It is part of me. I dream about it, I sacrifice and suffer for it, I live for it, and I would gladly die for it. Go forward come what may."

ADRIFT IN THE WORLD

The UNIA was never the same again. The American membership had always been the mainstay of the organization, and without Garvey's leadership, the movement began to die. To the end of his life, Garvey tried desperately to recapture the magic of 1920, but he was hopelessly handicapped by his banishment abroad.

Garvey was philosophical about his misfortunes in the United States and was always hopeful about the future: "I never look back, there is no time for that, besides, it would make me cautious."

When the news that Garvey was returning reached Jamaica, his countrymen flocked to the Kingston pier to greet the *Santa Marta*, which he had boarded in Panama. Garvey had become a hero to Jamaican blacks, and crowds lined the streets to watch him make his triumphant way to the local UNIA headquarters. He had come a long way since his quiet departure from the island 11 years earlier.

Garvey immediately began to rebuild the long-neglected Jamaican branch of the UNIA. He also made a valiant effort to maintain contact with his American followers, cabling his editorials to *Negro World* in New York every week. Determined to sustain the growth of the association, he traveled to England in the spring of 1928 to set up a European chapter of the UNIA. He was disappointed to find that blacks there showed little interest in the movement.

Shortly after Garvey arrived in London, he planned a meeting to explain his program. Certain that he could attract a huge audience, he rented the Royal Albert Hall, which had a seating capacity of 10,000. For weeks before the meeting, he sent out handbills and invitations. Only a few hundred people showed up for Garvey's lecture on the night of June 6, 1928, and he was deeply embarrassed. He gave a long, rambling speech in which he attacked his many enemies for sabotaging his great plans.

Quickly recovering from this setback, Garvey established a European headquarters for the UNIA in London and set up another branch in Paris. He then traveled to Canada, where he ran into more trouble with U.S. authorities. In Montreal, he made speeches urging American blacks to vote for the Democratic candidate, Alfred E. Smith, in the upcoming presidential election. When the American consul heard about Garvey's comments, he complained to Canadian officials. Garvey was asked to leave the country.

Early in 1929, Garvey returned to Jamaica. Always planning ahead, he began thinking about the upcoming summer and the traditional August convention. Only one convention had been held after 1923, and that had been an emergency meeting called by UNIA officers while Garvey was in prison. Now that he was free, he wanted to call the world's black community together once again. Since he could not go to the traditional convention site in Harlem, he decided that the delegates must come to him. The Sixth International Convention of the Negro Peoples of the World was scheduled to be held in Kingston that August.

The 1929 convention was truly a reminder of the glorious days of the UNIA's peak. On the opening day, thousands of cheering spectators lined the streets of Kingston to view a parade that stretched for five miles. Men, women, and children perched on rooftops, fences, and trees to watch the amazing spectacle. Garvey, wearing scarlet robes and a red and white hat, rode in an open car that was decorated with the UNIA colors of red, black, and green. Around him marched the uniformed members of the UNIA's various divisions. At the end of the parade were grouped the thousands of delegates who had again answered Garvey's call.

Garvey was triumphant. The convention reassured him that his organizational skills and leadership talents were still intact. Unfortunately, the 1929 convention was also the scene of trouble between the UNIA leader and the organization's U.S. chapters. Early in the month-long convention Garvey criticized some of the American UNIA leaders. It was their fault, Garvey charged, that the organization faltered while he was in prison. Stung by these accusations, the Americans grew hostile to Garvey. When he demanded that the UNIA's international headquarters be moved from New York to Kingston, they rebelled.

Garvey, as the founder and president of the association, wanted the headquarters to be where he was. The Americans, protesting that the UNIA's strength and financial support were based in the United States, wanted it to remain in New York. Unwilling to compromise on the issue, the U.S. delegates angrily withdrew from the convention.

Because the U.S. branch of the association had accumulated some heavy debts, Garvey was eager to sever his ties and start anew. The split became official in August 1929. Garvey renamed his group the Parent Body of the Universal Negro Improvement Association. Both the American organization and Garvey's international association continued to refer to themselves as the UNIA. The schism further weakened his already faltering movement.

Meanwhile, Garvey decided to try his hand at Jamaican politics. In 1929, he formed the People's Political party and began campaigning for a seat in the Jamaican legislature. His platform called for an improvement in working conditions and economic and educational opportunities for Jamaican blacks. He also called for a reform of the judiciary system. After making negative remarks about certain Jamaican judges, he was sentenced to three months in jail for contempt of court. He served a few terms on the local governing council of Kingston, but the People's Political Party was never a great success. While he was in Jamaica, he became the father of two sons: Marcus, born in 1930, and Julius, born in 1933.

THE END OF THE MAN AND THE MOVEMENT

In 1935, Garvey left Jamaica for the last time and moved the UNIA headquarters to London. His efforts to rebuild his once-great organization from Jamaica had failed. He hoped that in London he would have better luck.

A few months after Garvey arrived in London he was heart-broken by the news that the independent black nation of Ethiopia had been attacked and invaded by Italy. His hope for black self-rule in Africa grew weaker after Ethiopia's conquest. Although he joined other black spokesmen in denouncing Italy's unprovoked attack, he also criticized Ethiopia's ruler, Emperor Haile Selassie, for failing to modernize the country's armed forces so that they could repel the invasion. (For additional information on the invasion of Ethiopia, enter "Ethiopia invasion by Italy" into any search engine and browse the sites listed.)

Garvey called on the world's blacks to unite in defense of their ancestral homeland and predicted grim consequences if they failed. "This is a warning," he said of Ethiopia's defeat. "If you Negroes do not readjust and steady yourselves and think intelligently as the age demands, your next fifty years will not see you defeated but will see you wiped out entirely from civilization."

Using his newest publication, a monthly magazine called *Black Man* that he had started in December 1933, Garvey published his views on the Ethiopian situation and other black issues. *Negro World* had folded in 1933, and Garvey knew he needed some way to keep in touch with his scattered followers. *Black Man* was expensive to publish and distribute and appeared less frequently as the years went on.

Garvey tried to regain a following in the United States, and he held UNIA conferences in Toronto, Canada, in 1936, 1937, and 1938. Some loyal Garveyites crossed the Canadian border to see their old leader, but their numbers grew fewer each year.

Realizing that he needed to recruit the younger generation if he wanted to keep the movement going, in 1937 Garvey formed the School of African Philosophy to train interested students for UNIA leadership. The program was offered as a correspondence course, but only eight students enrolled in the school in 1937.

Ultimately, Garvey's efforts to rebuild the UNIA failed. The membership dwindled, and from 1935 to 1937 Garvey collected less than $400 from all of his various fund-raising drives. The days when he could raise thousands of dollars in a single night were gone forever. He was barely able to support his family and could not afford to bring them to England until the summer of 1937. The wet and chilly English climate was hard on his two sons, however, and in 1938 Amy Jacques Garvey took the boys back to Jamaica. Garvey remained behind.

Garvey had presided over a wealthy organization during the UNIA's heyday, but he lived close to poverty during his final years. He had never accepted the full salaries due him as president of the UNIA and the Black Star Line, and he had often used his own savings for organizational activities. Garvey often wrote to his family, assuring them that the association would take care of them after he died. "I have nothing to leave for them, but the service I have cheerfully given to my race will guarantee their future," he believed.

In January 1940, Garvey suffered a serious stroke that left his right side paralyzed. He had always had a problem with asthma, and he suffered two dangerous bouts of pneumonia during the 1930s. Garvey's doctor urged him to leave England for the warmer Jamaican climate, but he refused. He knew he could not lead an international organization from that tiny, isolated island.

Sick as Garvey was, he continued to conduct UNIA business from his home. He read all of his letters and newspapers, dictated correspondence, and held interviews at his bedside. In May 1940, the final blow came. A London newspaper published a report that Garvey had died in poverty. Believing the story to be true, other newspapers picked up the story and printed obituaries. Cables and condolence letters poured into Garvey's London office. His secretary, fearing the effect that this depressing correspondence would have on his frail health, kept the mail and newspapers from him for several days.

Garvey finally grew suspicious and demanded to know what was going on. He was given his mail, but the shock of reading his own obituary was too much for him. "When he saw the black streamer headlines of the Negro newspapers, he motioned to [his secretary] that he wanted to dictate a statement; but he cried aloud in anguish, and fell back into his pillow. He was unable to speak again," wrote Amy Jacques Garvey, reporting the news she heard from her husband's friends in London.

Garvey died on June 10, 1940, at the age of 53. His last request was that his body be brought back to Jamaica from the "land of strangers." More than two decades later, that request was honored. In 1964, Garvey's remains were transported to his homeland by the Jamaican government. Garvey, once scorned by the Jamaican elite, was given the title of "First National Hero," the country's highest honor.

GARVEY'S LEGACY

Although Garvey's name is not widely known today, his ideas live on. During the decades after his death, much of Africa won freedom. Garvey never visited the land that played such a large role in his dreams, but his philosophy had a profound impact on that continent. Many leaders of the emerging black nations, such as Nnamdi Azikiwe of Nigeria and Kwame Nkrumah of Ghana, have acknowledged the importance of

Garvey died in England on June 10, 1940, and over twenty years later his remains were moved to this gravesite in Kingston, Jamaica. Though Garvey's life was marred by controversy and he is not as widely known today as other black leaders, his philosophy and his support of black pride continue to have significant influence on black leaders and thinkers.

Garvey's movement in their fight for independence. Nkrumah said, "I think that of all the literature I studied, the book that did more to fire my enthusiasm was the *Philosophy and Opinions of Marcus Garvey.*"

Garvey's philosophy has had a lasting influence on the United States. During the 1960s, young black Americans dissatisfied with the progress of the civil rights movement revived many of his ideas. Like Garvey, these militant young people advocated black separatism and self-reliance. "Black power" became their rallying cry.

Many black leaders cited Garvey as a major influence on their lives; one was Malcolm X, who in the 1960s was the spokesman of the black separatist organization known as the Nation of Islam. Malcolm's father was a passionate Garveyite, and, as a young boy, Malcolm was exposed to Garvey's doctrine of African nationalism and black unity. "Every time you see another nation on the African continent become independent, you know Marcus Garvey is alive," Malcolm X once said. "All the freedom movements that are taking place right here in America today were initiated by the work and teachings of Marcus Garvey."

Garvey's ideas provided Malcolm X with an ideological starting point, and Garvey's insistence on quiet dignity and impeccable public behavior on the part of his UNIA followers served as an example of how to project both strength and firm purpose. The Nation of Islam's emphasis on economic self-sufficiency and the pervasive Afrocentrism that characterized its worldview clearly bore Garvey's imprint.

Garvey and UNIA also reappeared in a different way under the trademark black berets of the Black Panther Party. Like Garvey, leaders of the most famous black militant group of the 1960s, such as Huey Newton, stressed not only the economic independence of the black community but also collective self-defense. The Black Panthers never advocated a return to Africa, but the call of black pride that they broadcast echoed Garvey's earlier appeals. Like the crisp suits and razor-sharp bow ties of members of the Nation of Islam, the berets and leather coats of the Black Panthers offered a new image of uniformed African Americans determined to advance racial solidarity and justice—just as UNIA had done decades earlier. There is no denying the debt owed to Garvey by late-twentieth-century radicals who consciously or unconsciously resurrected his tactics and style.

Garvey's ideas are reflected in the words and actions of many of the black activists who followed him. Regardless of their opinions of Garvey himself, black leaders—conservatives and radicals—could ignore neither the man nor his message.

Themes of black pride and a global black agenda resonate today and testify to the enduring legacy of Marcus Garvey.

The black newspaper *Amsterdam News* described Garvey's accomplishments in this way: "Marcus Garvey made black people proud of their race. In a world where black is despised, he taught them that black is beautiful."

Garvey knew that the fight would continue after his death. "When I am dead wrap the mantle of the Red, Black and Green around me," he once said. "Look for me in the whirlwind or the storm, look for me all around you, for, with God's grace, I shall come and bring with me countless millions of black slaves who have died in America and the West Indies and the millions in Africa to aid you in the fight for Liberty, Freedom and Life."

1887 Born Marcus Mosiah Garvey in St. Ann's Bay, Jamaica, on August 17

1917 Establishes the New York branch of UNIA

1918 *Negro World* begins publication

1919 UNIA goes into business as the United Negro Factories Corporation and the Black Star Line; Garvey marries Amy Ashwood

1920 Presides over the First International Convention of the Negro Peoples of the World

1921 Travels to Latin America; U.S. government tries to prevent his return; African Orthodox Church is founded

1922 Divorces Amy Ashwood; marries Amy Jacques; later is arrested, charged, and indicted for mail fraud in connection with Black Star Line; meets with Ku Klux Klan members

1923 Convicted in mail fraud trial and sentenced to five years imprisonment; he appeals his conviction and is released on bail

1924 Black Cross Navigation and Trading Company is set up

1925 Appeals are rejected; enters the Atlanta Penitentiary

1927 Sentence is commuted; is deported to Jamaica

1928 Travels to London; European UNIA branch founded

1929 Returns to Jamaica and presides over Sixth International Convention of the Negro Peoples of the World

1930 Marcus, Jr., is born; another son, Julius Winston, is born three years later

1935 Moves UNIA headquarters to London

1940 Dies in London on June 10

Clarke, John Henrick, ed. *Marcus Garvey and the Vision of Africa.* New York: Random House, 1974.

Cronon, E. David. *Black Moses: The Story of Marcus Garvey and the Universal Negro Improvement Association.* Madison: University of Wisconsin Press, 1969.

Davis, Daniel S. *Marcus Garvey.* New York: Franklin Watts, 1972.

Garvey, Amy Jacques. *Garvey and Garveyism.* Kingston, Jamaica: United Printers, 1963.

Garvey, Amy Jacques, ed. *Philosophy and Opinions of Marcus Garvey.* New York: Atheneum, 1986.

Hill, Robert A., ed. *The Marcus Garvey and Universal Negro Improvement Association Papers.* Berkeley: University of California Press, 1983.

Martin, Tony. *Marcus Garvey, Hero: A First Biography.* Dover, MA: Majority Press, 1983.

————. *Race First: The Ideological and Organizational Struggles of Marcus Garvey and the Universal Negro Improvement Association.* Dover, MA: Majority Press, 1976.

Nembhard, Len S. *Trials and Triumphs of Marcus Garvey.* New York: Kraus Reprint Company, 1978.

WEBSITES

About Marcus Garvey
http://afroamhistory.about.com/cs/marcusgarvey/p/bio_garvey.htm

American Experience
http://www.pbs.org/wgbh/amex/garvey/

Encarta Africana

http://www.africana.com/research/encarta/tt_608.asp

Harlem: 1900–1940

http://www.si.umich.edu/CHICO/Harlem/text/garvey.html

page:

3: © Lake Country Museum/
CORBIS

7: © Hulton\Archive by
Getty Images, Inc.

14: Library of Congress

19: Library of Congress

29: © David J. & Janice L. Frent
Collection/CORBIS

36: © CORBIS

45: © Underwood & Underwood/
CORBIS

48: © Underwood & Underwood/
CORBIS

52: Library of Congress

62: Library of Congress

69: © Bettmann/CORBIS

73: © Bettmann/CORBIS

80: © Jacques M. Chenet/CORBIS

Cover: © Underwood & Underwood/CORBIS

ABOUT THE AUTHOR

Mary Lawler is a freelance writer living in New York. She is a graduate of Duke University and has also studied at the University of Copenhagen, Denmark. She is a former reporter for the *Brookline Citizen* in Brookline, Massachusetts

AUTHOR OF ADDITIONAL TEXT, LEGACY EDITION

John Davenport holds a Ph.D. from the University of Connecticut and currently teaches at Corte Madera School in Portola Valley, California. He lives in San Carlos, California, with his wife Jennifer, and his two sons, William and Andrew. He has previously written *The U.S.-Mexico Border* and *The Mason-Dixon Line* in the Chelsea House series ARBITRARY BORDERS.

CONSULTING EDITOR, REVISED EDITION

Heather Lehr Wagner is a writer and editor. She is the author of 30 books exploring social and political issues and focusing on the lives of prominent Americans and has contributed to biographies of Frederick Douglass, Harriet Tubman, Sojourner Truth, Malcolm X, Thurgood Marshall, and Martin Luther King, Jr., in the revised BLACK AMERICANS OF ACHIEVEMENT series. She earned a BA in political science from Duke University and an MA in government from the College of William and Mary. She lives with her husband and family in Pennsylvania.

CONSULTING EDITOR, FIRST EDITION

Nathan Irvin Huggins was W.E.B. Du Bois Professor of History and Director of the W.E.B. Du Bois Institute for Afro-American Research at Harvard University. He previously taught at Columbia University. Professor Huggins was the author of numerous books, including *Black Odyssey: The Afro-American Ordeal in Slavery*, *The Harlem Renaissance*, and *Slave and Citizen: The Life of Frederick Douglass*. Nathan I. Huggins died in 1989.